This book would never have been written without my parents, **Roger and Joy Martin, Sr**. There is the obvious reason: I would not have been born. There are the reasons you wouldn't know. Dad and Mom taught me a love of reading and an appreciation for learning...from everyone. Our home was a greenhouse for the discussion of ideas, from the wildest weeds to the grandest flowers. Whatever grace you pick from this book has its root in their humble and teachable spirit.

I love you, Mom and Dad.

PARTLY WRONG

PARTLY WRONG

Admit it. Embrace it. Live it.

Roger Martin, Jr.

Find Our Way Home Press

Copyright 2018 by Roger Martin, Jr.
All rights reserved.

Printed in the United States of America

ISBN 978-1-7327359-0-3

First printing, 2018

The author may be contacted through:
rogermartinjr.com
Findourwayhomepress@gmail.com

Cover design by germancreative (a Fiverr partner)

Contents

Contents, continued

Introduction

My first title for the book was "Partly Right," but I decided against it, having learned that Anthony Campolo authored a book with that title. I'm glad I did. For me, "Partly Wrong" is more engaging, uncomfortable and accurate. Thanks, Mr. Campolo!

I hope no one is shocked to learn that they're partly wrong. I hope we're challenged to see that we don't act like it nearly enough. I hope we're moved to make changes. I'm impressed you're considering a book with an uncomfortable title and premise.

I'm a follower of Jesus whose life has been radically changed by Jesus' life and the wisdom of the Bible. And so you'll find me appealing to the Bible often as an authority. Every key idea here traces back to its wisdom. Most Bible references are from the New International Version.

At the end of the book, you'll find discussion questions that encourage personal reflection or group discussion for each chapter of the book.

Scanning through the chapter titles, you may find yourself immediately drawn to read one or two of them first. The chapters may, of course, be read in any order, but the first four chapters provide the foundational ideas that are practically expanded throughout, so you may find it helpful to read them first.

The dilemma of writing a book that claims that we're all partly wrong is obvious. I may be wrong. I'll say some things right things, and I'll say some wrong things. I only wish I knew which ones were which. You'll have the adventure of figuring that out. Have fun.

I'm honored you're reading.

Roger

Chapter One

***

IT SUCKS TO BE WRONG

"Huge Lot of Comics and Baseball Memorabilia."

The Craigslist ad title screamed at me. It was 2004. Only
3 years earlier, I had discovered--and joined--this
intriguing 6-year old website with a weird name, eBay.
The platform was fascinating, and I tried my hand at
selling a few things. Some old radios a neighbor threw out.
Boxes of overstock Hallmark ornaments. A huge lot of
vintage Broadway playbills someone was giving away on

Freecycle.org. I made some pretty good sales, and I wanted to make more.

Some of my best sales were "hidden treasures," something of value that was being tossed out. I paid almost nothing for it, but I made quite a profit. That's the attraction of selling on eBay. You tell yourself that you're just looking for some good things to sell. The truth is that you're always looking for "the big one." The picture with some ancient American government document tucked away in the frame. The video game every collector is dying to have. The crappy old snare drum that turns out to be a Ludwig "Black Beauty." The baseball card that's one of only four known to exist.

The word "baseball" in the ad got my attention. Suddenly, I could feel my heart beating. I dialed the seller, casually asking about the ad. No, the lot hadn't sold yet, but a lot of people were calling about it. Of course, I could come see it. Why yes, he could even work me in for a visit today. I scribbled down the address, jumped in my van and drove to his town 35 minutes northwest of us. Inching down a two lane road, searching mailbox numbers, I found his drive and turned in. The van followed a dusty gravel road to a large rustic barn just past the main house.

A wiry man in his late fifties greeted me with a handshake and smile. Was that a twinkle in his eye...or a glint? I followed him up the back stairs to a loft door. Stepping in out of the sun, I squinted in the darkness. Slowly, box after box after box began to appear on dusty shelves, on tables, on the floor.

"Take your time and look around. Somebody else called and wants to come look at them after a bit."

I'd better hurry. Where to start? There were endless boxes of sleeved comic books. Dusty boxes held tens of thousands of baseball cards, many indexed by years. I saw a signed baseball or two. Hmm. Looks like "Mickey Mantle" on that baseball. A dusty table displayed some really old looking baseball cards—an odd size—unlike anything I'd seen before. Interesting names. Wow. Honus Wagner. I've heard that name somewhere before. That card looks really old. A couple of creases on it, but what if? And beyond this handful of odd rectangular cards, there were comics and cards everywhere I scanned.

So why was he selling, I asked. He chuckled. Something about his wife wanting it all out of here, wanting to fix up the house. That sounded legitimate. I ventured a question about the price. It was, he quickly reminded, a remarkable collection. The cost was $2,500. Good gosh. I didn't have that kind of money sitting around. Four children at home will do that to you. Maybe he'd consider something less.

"Well, if you buy it today, I'd sell it for $2,000. We have to get it out of here. And I have a box truck I could load it in and take it to your house."

The deal dangled in the air. My thoughts bounced like pinballs. There were other callers asking about the ad. Honus Wagner. EBay. I could go to a nearby bank and get a cash advance off my credit card. I should probably call my wife, Joy, before borrowing that amount of money. Tens of thousands of cards. Mickey Mantle. Sleeved comic books by the case. Really old cards. Honus Wagner. You know, there's no need to worry Joy with all that stressful financial stuff. Maybe she won't ask what it cost anyway. There's a signed Mickey Mantle. You've done great on eBay. It's a huge risk, but what if... ?

Two hours later, a truck pulled into our driveway, and the seller and I proceeded to fill my garage with a "Huge Lot of Comics and Baseball Memorabilia."

My kids were curious, so I told them the story about my amazing deal. Joy was curious, so I told her how her eBay husband had found this sporting treasure. How much did it cost? Well, it's some really, really cool stuff. Oh look, I think I see a deer in the backyard.

I couldn't wait to research my treasure. The initial information was encouraging. Those odd rectangular cards were tobacco cards which, decades ago, were included in packs of cigarettes. They featured various sports figures, including Honus Wagner. An original "T206 Honus Wagner" tobacco card, even in poor condition, will pay off your house mortgage. The word "original" is significant. I soon discovered the unsettling reality known as reproductions.

I researched and studied and put the cards under a microscope and read some more, discovering what you have guessed by now. My tobacco cards were not originals. The comics were originals and in great condition, but the comic market had just taken quite a tumble. They looked more valuable than they were. I had tens of thousands of baseball cards, but only tens of them had any reasonable value. The most valuable ones of them weren't in the sets. That's odd. I wonder how that could've happened?

After dozens of hours of research, creating eBay listings

and negotiating with an out-of-state collector, I sold everything for a total of $987. That's right. I forfeited hours and hours of time with my kids in order to lose more than $1,000, money we desperately needed for other things. I felt really stupid.

I was wrong...really wrong...on many levels.

I was wrong about the value of the baseball memorabilia. I was wrong about how much I knew. I was wrong about hiding the purchase from my wife. I was wrong about not getting counsel from someone who could have helped me evaluate the "amazing" deal.

I've been wrong about many things. In fact, the subtitle of this book could be "Endlessly Entertaining Stories of Roger's Errors and Ineptitude." I'm wrong, and I've been wrong, about things far more important than baseball cards and comics.

Of course, I've also been right before. I am dying to tell you about some impressive eBay sales I've made. Sometimes I make a right judgment. Sometimes I believe the right idea. Sometimes I do the right thing. Sometimes I say the right thing to my wife. Sometimes.

So I'm partly right.

Which is another way of saying that I am partly wrong.

I don't know about you, but I hate being wrong. I hate being ignorant. I hate looking silly or stupid. I hate making choices that hurt other people. I hate guiding people in the wrong direction. I hate making mistakes. I hate blind spots. I hate speaking words that wound my children or my wife. I hate admitting that I'm wrong. I hate people knowing that I am wrong.

Being wrong is depressing, frustrating, embarrassing, and damaging. It divides, discourages, worries and burdens. I try to avoid it. I try to hide it. I try to fix it. I try to downplay it. Nothing good comes from being wrong. For most of my life, that is what I believed.

But I was wrong.

While reading the Bible recently, I listened in on a conversation Jesus had with his first followers, and a switch flipped. I noticed something I had walked right by dozens of times before. It launched a journey through the pages of the Bible that somehow made partly wrong feel more like a blessing than a curse. An opportunity rather than a liability. A gift from God rather than an obstacle for

God. This theme permeates the Bible.

Listening to the biblical narrative and assessing my own experience, here is what I have come to believe:

Partly wrong can't be avoided, and that's all right.
Partly wrong is the soil in which grace, love and humility grow best..
Partly wrong opens the door for deeper relationships and community.
Partly wrong is the classroom for learning and growth
Partly wrong creates unexpected opportunities for God to bless others through you.
Partly wrong gives you credibility and hope when talking to someone about Jesus.
Partly wrong answers some perplexing questions.
Partly wrong is often what God uses to get us right.

I'm aware of the tension I raise with these claims. I'm partly wrong. Part of what I say in this book will be right, and part will be wrong. I just don't know which is which. I'm inviting you, then, into a reading journey in which you wrestle with where I'm wrong and where I'm right. You could even make an adventure of it, scanning my words for the places where I'm wrong. You could pencil a "W" next to a wrong statement and an "R" next to a right one. Pencil in hand or not, I invite you to read and to wrestle with a "partly wrong" paradigm that has produced unexpected freedom, joy, clarity and growth for me. I hope it does the same for you.

So, what's that Jesus conversation that changed my entire view of being wrong?

PARTLY WRONG

Chapter Two

***

IT ROCKS TO BE RIGHT

It's fun to be right.

It's even more fun when people know that you're right.

I spent about 19 years in school, and it's impossible to know how many times I sat in a classroom when the teacher asked the class a question, expecting one of us to raise our hand and give an answer. Sometimes the teacher would ask a specific person to answer the question. I can still see the teacher scanning the room to decide who would be the chosen one.

Some students dreaded the teacher's scan, avoiding eye contact at all costs. I wanted to be called. My hand would shoot up. Sometimes, I waved. Yes, I was one of *those* people. Some of it was arrogance and foolishness, I know, but I think another part was the "Jeopardy Show" effect, the challenge of facing down the Alex Trebek question. The risk, of course, was that I could get the dreaded "oh no!" from Alex or my teacher, but the potential reward was getting the "that's right," and all the better that others were around to witness my great moment, my right-ness.

So, it's hard for me not to think of Alex Trebek and the Jeopardy Show when I read one of the fascinating Jesus stories in the Bible. Jesus is traveling around with his little "class" of twelve students known simply as disciples. And from time to time, he'd ask the class a question.

"When Jesus came to the region of Caesarea Philippi, he asked his disciples, 'Who do people say the Son of Man is?' They replied, 'Some say John the Baptist; others say Elijah; and still others, Jeremiah or one of the prophets.'" (Matthew 16:13-14)

Who do people say the "son of Man is?" Or "Who do people say that I am?" This was a safe question, meaning that there was no "right" or "wrong" answer. Everyone piped in with possible answers. Having heard what they' overheard from others, Jesus now asked the "unsafe" question.

"'But what about you?' he asked. 'Who do you say I am?'" *(vs. 15)*

Now things got interesting...and quieter, I expect. I'm pretty certain some of the disciples reflexively glanced toward Peter. He was the one who loved these kinds of moments, that kid in the class raising and waving his hand. Sure enough, Peter spoke up.

"You are the Messiah, the Son of the living God." (vs. 16)

Now, the other disciples turned back to Jesus to see if Peter would get the "oh no" or the "yes!" They didn't have to wait long.

"Jesus replied, 'Blessed are you, Simon son of Jonah, for this was not revealed to you by flesh and blood, but by my Father in heaven.'" (vss. 16-17)

Wow! This wasn't just a "you're right." This was a "you nailed it!" On occasion, I've had those moments in a classroom, so I know that Peter had to be beaming, subtly glancing at the others to see their response. I see the other disciples high-fiving him, when Jesus interrupted with another word to Peter.

"'And I tell you that you are Peter, and on this rock I will build my church, and the gates of Hades will not overcome it. I will give you the keys of the kingdom of heaven; whatever you bind on earth will be bound in heaven, and whatever you loose on earth will be loosed in heaven.'" (vss. 18-19)

It kept getting better. This was like the teacher following up your right answer with a prediction about your future. "You've got what it takes to be a CEO, to be a general, to be the President." Jesus called Peter a rock. He affirmed that Peter would be part of the foundation of His church in the world. "You're going places. I'm going to work through your life in a great way."

Can this classroom moment possibly get any better? So, if you were Peter in this moment, how would you feel? What would be going on in your heart?

***

Well, it turns out that the class wasn't over yet. Jesus still had a bit more teaching to do.

"From that time on Jesus began to explain to his disciples that he must go to Jerusalem and suffer many things at the hands of the elders, the chief priests and the teachers of the law, and that he must be killed and on the third day be raised to life." (vs. 21)

Well, the first part of the class had been swell. The disciples learned that Jesus was the Son of God, the chosen Messiah, and they were his best friends and students. Do the math. This should work out quite nicely for "the disciples." Jesus was going to build something great, and Peter (along with his companions) was going to be right in the middle of it. Awesome....until Jesus changed the tone entirely and told them that He MUST suffer and be killed and be raised to life. This was too much for Peter.

"Peter took him aside and began to rebuke him. 'Never, Lord!' he said. 'This shall never happen to you!'" (vss. 21-22)

Jesus wasn't really asking for an answer on this one; Peter just volunteered one! Hey, when you get a classroom answer correct, you feel much more confident about offering answers the next time. Peter was suddenly feeling like "answer man." All this talk about Jesus being killed was obviously wrong; He must let Jesus in on this. To Peter's credit, he pulled Jesus off to the side, perhaps not wanting to publicly rebuke him. "Jesus, this talk about you being killed...uh, it's never going to happen...never!"

I don't know exactly what he expected Jesus to say, how he saw this going in his mind. It has always seemed comical to imagine Peter telling Jesus He's wrong—especially after just declaring that Jesus is the Son of the living God. Maybe he thought Jesus would look at him wistfully and say, "You're right; I was mistaken on that one, Peter." That's not how it went down.

Jesus turned and said to Peter, "Get behind me, Satan! (vs. 23)

My loose translation of Jesus' words here: You're wrong, Peter—really, really wrong! Peter had to be dumbstruck. That nickname, "the rock," was pretty cool, but this new name, Satan? Sounds a bit harsh. Man, I feel for Peter. I also know the feeling of getting an answer terribly wrong.

Unfortunately, Peter's correction wasn't finished. It was awesome when Jesus kept praising his right answer, but it had to be hard for the correction of the wrong answer to continue.

"You are a stumbling block to me; you do not have in mind the concerns of God, but merely human concerns." *(vs. 23)*

Jesus was wonderfully, brutally honest. "You do not have in mind the concerns of God." And here we encounter an odd but significant tension that became the seed of this book. In one moment, Jesus tells Peter that he's right, that God Himself has opened his eyes to a truth that many others have not yet seen. In the next moment, Jesus tells this very same Peter that he's wrong, that He doesn't have in mind the concerns of God. Peter is right, but he's also wrong. Peter is actively hearing from God, but he also doesn't have in mind the things of God. Peter is being used by God, but Peter is also being used by the great enemy, Satan. In the same moment.

Peter is partly wrong. Peter is partly right. Peter believes some right ideas that come from God Himself. Peter believes some wrong ideas that come from Satan Himself. Peter sees some things correctly. Peter sees some things incorrectly. Peter is behaving in some ways that honor God. Peter is behaving in some ways that grieve God. Peter is in that same moment right and wrong. Partly wrong.

And Peter's story is our story.

We are—all of us, in this very moment—partly right and partly wrong. And God wants to do good work in the world through us. Think about what Jesus said to Peter. He would be a rock, and God would use his life and his declaration and his words to build the church, this centerpiece of God's work in the world. And he was. Peter was used by God in a remarkable way even though he was partly wrong, and continued to be. How could it be any less true for us?

And here is the kicker. God planned it that way! The pages of the Bible unfold an unexpected pattern. God is at work *through* our partly wrong, not in spite of it. Peter was not an aberration; He was the prototype. He exemplifies how God works in our partly wrong world. Your partly wrong opens the door for God to do a world of good through you.

If you will let him.

You'll have to live with your partly wrong in a different way. Being right is not everything; it can actually move your heart away from God at times. Partly wrong is an opportunity. Partly wrong is not something to hide or deny or disguise. It is something to remember and acknowledge and entrust to God for good. Partly wrong is what God uses to get you right.

Understanding your partly wrong--and the good God wants to do through it--will nurture an unexpected but welcome reality. Freedom. The fight to constantly be right and look right is an impossible burden. Embracing your partly wrong and entrusting it to God frees you from the relentless pursuit of right-ness.

I understand if you are skeptical. The narrative I am unpacking is very different from the story I've believed most of my life. If you'll let me, I'd love to unpack the story a bit further in the chapters ahead. By the way, what do you know about lug nuts?

Chapter Three

***

I DID NOT SEE THAT COMING

I have moved from one house to another...a lot. By my count, I have lived in 19 different houses, meaning I've moved 18 times in 56 years. I consider myself a bit of an expert. Let me tell you a fun story about move number 16, a move that took my family from Alabama to Massachusetts.

Moving reality #1 is this: you always have more stuff than you think you have. Related reality: your stuff expands to

fill the size of your storage space. This is an immutable
law of the universe. So, when the time has come to box up
and pack up my stuff for a move, I've never said: "Gee, we
have less stuff than I thought." Just the opposite. It's some
form of, "I can't believe we have this much stuff." So for
this move, I decided we'd need not only a 48-foot U-Haul
truck, but also a 12-foot utility trailer, which I purchased
new a day before our move.

As I drove the trailer home from the store, a tire went flat.
This is never a good sign. Don't get me started on the
Martin "tire curse!" I had to replace a tire on a brand new
trailer! Maybe you know the routine: loosen the lug nuts,
pull off the lug nuts, put on the new tire, put the lug nuts
back on, and tighten the lug nuts. The next day, we loaded
everything that wouldn't fit in the truck on the trailer,
aaaaand we still had to leave some stuff behind. You can
only imagine how much we piled on that trailer.

The next morning, we left on our venture. I was driving the
truck, my wife was driving a van with the kids, and my
friend, Brad, was driving our Isuzu pickup, also piled high
with stuff. Our first stop would be Chattanooga, about two
hours away. An hour or so into our trip, I had this
innocent little thought cross my mind: Did I tighten those
lug nuts after I replaced that tire on the trailer? I could not

remember, but then I thought: I'll check it when we get to Chattanooga. Another hour can't hurt anything.

I continued driving, tooling along at about 65 mph. As planned, we stopped in Chattanooga for supper. I forgot about the tire entirely until we were getting ready to drive away again. I climbed out of the vehicle to check the left tire's lug bolts...more specifically, what was left of them. I was stunned.

I had NOT tightened those lug nuts! In that short "little" two hour drive, the lug nuts had worked themselves very loose, allowing the tire to jiggle on the lug bolts, an action which ground out the rim holes, through which the lug bolts secured the tire to the axle. The rim holes were actually larger now than the lug nuts. This is the simpler version: Nothing was securing the tire to the axle. Jack up the trailer, and the tire would simply have fallen off.

We were seconds from a disaster that could've taken out any vehicle following us, including the one driven by my wife. And why? I was partly wrong.

I was mistaken and didn't know it. I didn't know that loose lug nuts could loosen so quickly. I didn't know you could grind out tire rim holes to almost twice their original diameter. I didn't know that loose lug nuts could do so much damage in two hours that your tire could completely leave your vehicle. Now, I know. I gained some vital new knowledge that day. I grew in my knowledge. In fact, that's a big part of what growth is in almost every part of our lives.

Peter, the dear friend we met in our last chapter, made this interesting plea in the Bible:

"But grow in the grace and knowledge of our Lord and Savior Jesus Christ. To him be glory both now and forever! Amen." (2 Peter 3:18)

Grow in the grace and knowledge of our Lord. There's a passion in his words. Perhaps in this moment, he remembers his overconfidence about what he knew and the resulting attempt to correct Jesus. Keep learning from Jesus, he implores. Let him correct your partly wrongs. Another Bible writer, the apostle Paul, had this word to say about growing:

"For this reason, since the day we heard about you, we have not stopped praying for you. We continually ask God to fill you with the knowledge of his will through all the wisdom and understanding that the Spirit gives, so

*that you may live a life worthy of the Lord and please him
in every way: bearing fruit in every good work, growing
in the knowledge of God." (Colossians 1:9-10)*

Growing seems to be really important to God. Keep
growing. Never stop growing. Grow in grace. Grow in
knowledge. Add to your goodness, knowledge. The
Apostle Paul prayed daily that his friends and new
followers of Jesus would keep growing. As best I can see,
there's no point at which God expects us to stop growing.

We need to grow. All the time. Now, isn't that just
another way of saying that we are partly wrong? All the
time. Think about it. If we need to keep growing every
single day, it means that every day we have wrong ideas
and values and motives and behaviors and opinions that
need to be changed. People who are completely right, who
have no wrong beliefs or motives or behaviors or values—
they have no need to grow. But God clarifies that there are
no such people. Instead, He says we all need to keep
growing every single day. Conclusion: You and I are
always partly wrong, always needing to grow in our
knowledge. We have mistaken ideas about God and life
and people and wholeness that need to be changed, so God
says "keep growing."

"But Roger, maybe it's just that our ideas are incomplete, not necessarily wrong." I wrestled with that idea myself, but I'm not sure "incomplete" and "wrong" are actually two different things. Here's what I mean. Where my information or knowledge is incomplete, I invariably fill the incomplete information with inaccurate ideas. I'm not sure you can avoid this.

I had no idea that loose lug nuts could in two hours render a tire rim virtually useless, creating grave danger. Because I didn't know that reality, I substituted a fallacy: No significant damage or harm could be created in two hours. I actually thought that in my mind. My incomplete knowledge resulted in a wrong idea. I didn't know enough about lug nuts, which is another way of saying I was wrong about lug nuts.

I'm wrong about a lot of things. And that is exactly why God says I need to keep growing. Every time I see the word "grow" in the Bible, it reminds me that I'm partly wrong.

I am Peter, and so are you. We're partly wrong, but God wants to incrementally correct the "partly wrongs." And while we're here on earth, we'll always be growing. You'll never meet someone who's right on everything. That person would have no need to grow. You may meet people who think they're right on everything, even the person you see in the mirror, but they're wrong. Nobody gets to be completely right; we're all partly wrong all the time.

That is a good thing because God uses it to grow us. Do you believe that? It may take a while. The truth is, God has worked very hard to open my eyes to this reality. I wasn't a quick learner, but some moments are more teachable than others. It's amazing how much God can teach you with a Sunfish sailboat and a storm.

Chapter Four

***

IGNORANCE IS BLESS

There's something magical about sailing. I love the classic Christopher Cross song by that name, and I've always harbored a sailing fantasy. Imagine, then, the moment years ago, when I discovered someone on Craigslist was giving away a Sunfish sailboat. I snatched it up both for the thrill of sailing and the thrill of zero dollars. I was now the bona fide owner of a sailboat. I could see myself sitting in the sailboat, one hand on the rudder and the other hand holding a rope attached to something important, the wind blowing wildly through my hair. I was a sailor.

Not long after, I traveled with friends to Sebago Lake in Maine for a week of vacation together as families. This would provide my sailing moment. I brought the sailboat for its maiden voyage on the wild and unpredictable seas of Sebago. Having done some Google research on sailing, I now knew words like starboard and aft and jib and such. One fine morning, two friends, Brad and Warren, joined me for an exploratory trip. We eagerly climbed into the bobbing craft, paddle and snacks in hand. A dozen yards from shore, we practiced a few maneuvers to insure we could sail with the wind and into the wind. Satisfied with our skill, we headed out into the expansive lake, riding a decent breeze. Sailing was everything I dreamed it would be.

Before long, the breeze was breezier, pushing us further from shore. It was time to head back into the wind, something we'd done easily before. Our boat, however, was oddly unresponsive. Perhaps a stiffer wind, an overloaded boat, and water in the hull had something to do with it. No problem, of course, because I was a sailor with quality mates. However, in wrestling with the suddenly obstinate craft, we failed to see our only oar slip into the waters. I can still see that oar getting smaller—we unable to steer the boat toward it—until it vanished on the choppy horizon.

The wind was now creating waves, pushing us steadily from the shrinking shoreline. We were, of course, going to be able to turn this thing around, but there was a greater sense of urgency. The sky was darkening, and the lake, once full of dancing seacraft, was now nearly empty. At one point, a boatmate jumped into the water, grabbed the back of the boat and attempted to push the craft by kicking his legs. Yes, we tried that! Minutes later, we pulled his shivering frame back into the listing craft. Each futile attempt to head into the wind was exposing our ignorance and inability. I remember a particularly disturbing thought. Perhaps we should flag a craft for help.

About that time, a much larger sailboat glided effortlessly near us. The relaxed occupants were sipping wine as the wind pushed them toward their destination. I suddenly wanted to be in their boat. This was the perfect chance to ask for help: an idea, a suggestion, a hand. Only we didn't. We smiled and waved nonchalantly, as if we'd planned to bob helplessly in the waves.

Why is it so hard to say we don't know something, that we are in over our heads, that we need help? I'm pretty sure

I'm not the only one. I'm in a conversation with someone who is repairing his car, and he mentions a solenoid, something that sounds like a planet to me. I have no idea what it does. So, what do I do? I smile knowingly, and say, "I always hate it when the solenoid gives out." Really, Roger?

So, let me get this straight. I don't want this person to know that I don't know something, when he already knows I don't know things...lots of things...millions of things. I'm ignorant. About loads of things. And so are you. The problem is that we usually equate ignorant with dumb, so when we don't know something, we feel like we're stupid. I'm uncomfortable with the word "ignorant," as if it's an indictment, but it's just a reality. All of us are ignorant, even the most celebrated genius or Jeopardy Show champion. Not one of us could even handle all of the knowledge in the world; we don't have the brain capacity. We're all ignorant.

The Bible states what we all know intuitively: "We know in part." (1 Corinthians 13:9) We don't know it all. We know partly. We don't understand it all. We understand partly. But that's great news, and you know why? It opens countless opportunities for God to teach us something. Our ignorance—our partly-wrong-ness—should pull us like gravity to read or listen to the words of the Bible, where our ignorance will be reduced in the places that matter most.

And so the Bible songwriter, David, reminds us:

"The law of the LORD is perfect, reviving the soul. The statutes of the LORD are trustworthy, making wise the simple. The precepts of the LORD are right, giving joy to the heart. The commands of the LORD are radiant, giving light to the eyes." (Psalm 19:7-8)

Ignorant, we need knowledge. Partly wrong, we need correction. Simple, we need wisdom. Blind, we need light. This should drive us to God to learn from His knowledge and wisdom and character. He loves to teach the partly wrong, but He also wants us to learn from each other. Our ignorance creates a wonderful opportunity for a parent or friend or neighbor or even a stranger to teach us something.

Let's rewind my conversation with a friend about his car problem and the solenoid. Start the video again, and this time why don't I instead say something like: "Time out. A solenoid? What does that do, and how do you replace it?" I'll tell you what will happen. My friend's eyes will get a little brighter as he begins to explain something he knows to me. People love it. Of course they do. You do too. It feels really good to know something and get to explain it to someone else. Talk about a win-win situation. They get the joy of sharing their knowledge, and you get to be a little less ignorant.

Now, here's what happens when we disguise our ignorance. We rob ourselves of the chance to learn and we rob someone else of the chance to share their knowledge, all in an effort to make it look like we know everything, which no one believes anyway. As my friend, Fred, would say, "What the what?"

So, here's what I've begun doing. I actively look for opportunities where someone can teach me something I don't know. I seek out chances to admit my ignorance. Someone mentions an R.O.U.S. in casual conversation; I stop and ask them what that means. (Rodents Of Unusual Size, in case you're wondering.) I'm eating a meal at someone's home; I ask them how they fixed that particular dish and what's in it. I see someone working on something in their garage; I ask them what they're building or fixing. No one ever turns that kind of question down...unless, of course, what they're doing is illegal.

I recommend that you practice putting these three words together and speak them out loud: "I...don't...know." I would just practice saying it right now. No, seriously. Right now. Just say, "I don't know." Say it again. Try different inflections. See, that's not really so bad. Now throw in a "could you help me?" O.K., that may be pushing it.

So, what happened out on the wild Sebago sea? Well, as the clouds threatened to drop thunderbolts any moment, we spied a motorboat zipping by us toward our tiny shore. We began to wave wildly, shamelessly, eventually catching their attention only at the last minute. They came alongside, and we mumbled something about them possibly helping us get our boat to shore.

You know what? They loved the chance to help. They roped us to their vessel and towed us back toward our shore. As I recall, a hundred yards from shore, we asked if they'd release us to go in on our own from there. After all, there was no need for the family to see us being towed in to shore. They might worry! (Sigh. Perhaps we hadn't really learned our lesson after all.) Would they release us early? They laughed. I think their exact response was, "not a chance."

***

Not a chance. It's what some people would say if you asked them whether God could ever use them for good in the world. But I'm going to say that they're wrong, because God has the strangest employment policy that I've ever seen.

Chapter Five

***

THE BROKEN PEOPLE GOD USES

There was no chance God was going to do anything good through my life. I was certain. Most kids discover their sexuality in adolescence. Not me. I was a toddler. I can't tell you how it happened or when, only that it did. It brought the most amazing sensations. With the good feelings, however, came a shame that I couldn't name or explain or shake. I sensed the keen displeasure of God. Good kids didn't have those kinds of struggles. I was quite sure NO other kids did.

As I flailed into adolescence, the desires and the struggle got stronger, the shame deeper, and the sense of distance from God greater. The sexual desires felt entirely unmanageable. I was miserable, alternately promising God never to give in again and then confessing the latest failure...when I could even get up the heart to do so. I prayed the struggle would disappear. It seemed to grow. And then someone invented the internet. Sigh.

I was a struggling kid, and naturally no one knew that more keenly than I. I knew my thoughts, my fantasies, my attitudes, my feelings, and my desires...and my failings. At the same time, I loved God, and wanted for God to be able to do good work through my life like He had worked through people in the Bible, people like Moses, Esther, Peter, Paul and—well...Mary.

But that was not going to happen. I was *way* too broken. I was quite sure I couldn't have any sinful behaviors or attitudes in my life and be used by God. There was that disturbing word in the Bible: *"If I regard iniquity in my heart, the Lord will not hear me."* (Psalm 66:18, KJV) And if He wasn't hearing me, He certainly wasn't going to be doing any good work through my life. God works good through people who are all right. Didn't the preachers confirm that you had to be "right with God?"

So, as long as everything was confessed and tidied up with God, as long as I wasn't doing or thinking anything I shouldn't be, God could do good work through my life. I would actually try to recall if I'd confessed every wrong thing I'd done or thought in a day, to make sure I'd covered everything. One unconfessed flaw, one unacknowledged mistake, and I was a goner. Say hello to total uselessness.

It turns out that I was partly wrong...about everything. For starters, my conclusions didn't jibe with the stories of Moses and David and Peter or really anyone else in the Bible that God used for good. Think back to that classic partly wrong Peter moment. Peter declared that Jesus was "the Christ, the Son of the living God," and Jesus was fairly gushing in His response.

"And I tell you that you are Peter, and on this rock I will build my church, and the gates of Hades will not overcome it." (Matthew 16:18)

Whatever else Jesus meant, he seemed to be quite clear that "I'm going to use you in an extraordinary way." And He did. But just minutes later, Jesus was severely rebuking Peter, saying *"You are a stumbling block to me; you do not have in mind the concerns of God, but merely human concerns."* (vs. 23) Oh, and there's this other little thing. He called Peter "Satan." Uh oh. Isn't he the guy who is actively working against God?

So let me get this straight. God spoke a profound, life-giving word through Peter even though, in that very moment, he was missing a key part of God's heart. It's not just that he was mistaken. He was. But his heart was actually working against the ways and heart of God! He was mistaken...and sinful...and used by God in the very same moment.

And it's not like this was an isolated event. Peter would soon be arguing (again!) about whether he was the greatest of the disciples. And Peter would publicly deny Jesus hours after announcing he'd be willing to die for Jesus. And Peter would one day publicly disassociate himself from and embarrass his Gentile friends because of Jewish peer pressure. And...God would use Him all the while. Wow! And those are just *some* of the stories the Bible records.

There is Moses, the hot-headed, fearful, murderous, stammering, send-somebody-else-not-me rancher who wants to retire herding sheep. And God uses Him to save hundreds of thousands of lives and to be a spokesman for God to the most powerful man in the known world. There's Miriam—envious, power-grabbing, divisive—who leads with Moses and writes profound words and songs of praise to God. There's the racially bigoted Jonah who loves personal comfort more than people...and God just happens to use his message to move tens of thousands of people to repentance and trust in God.

And then there's possibly the most troubling personal story in all of the Bible about a man considered by many to be Israel's greatest king, David. King David. He led his nation to follow the ways of God. He wrote dozens, if not hundreds, of songs of praise to God, many of which God inspired as part of the Holy Bible. He's described by God as "a man after my own heart." Wow! That's all beautiful, but there's that little problem about him committing adultery with a friend's wife, lying to cover it up, and ordering a contract killing on his friend and several other soldiers in his own army. As one person has said, "it seems like all the Bible's 'good guys' are 'bad guys.'" He's right.

Some time ago, in conversation with a friend, I blurted out: "Of course, God uses screw-ups. It's all He's got to work with!" Think about it. We're all partly wrong. The Bible is clear that our character transformation is a process —a slow, incremental process— which means at this very moment, we have attitudes and behaviors and values that break God's heart. Learning the heart and ways of God comes in small "brick by brick" layers, which means that right now, all of us have some wrong beliefs that God has yet to correct. We broken, misguided, mistaken, partly-wrong people are all God has to work with. The 100% right, 100% good Jesus-follower does not exist. God has only ever used deeply mistaken and flawed people. I may be the poster child for this reality.

I could point you back to the moment a few years back when I realized with heartbreaking force that I'd spent most of my life entirely neglecting the plight of the poor— the losses, the injustices, and the systems exploiting them. I began to see how I myself was exploiting the vulnerability of the poor. Shocked, I discovered hundreds of God's instructions in the Bible about loving and blessing and fighting for justice for the poor, commands I had somehow—quite conveniently—missed or ignored for decades. Decades! And for two of those decades, I was a pastor, teaching people about the heart and the ways of God. People have told me how my life or my teachings have helped them to trust Jesus and to live out His heart, but for many of those years, I was badly mistaken about and sinfully negligent in regard to the plight of the poor.

But God used me anyway.

We're all partly wrong people, and that's the only kind of person through whom God can do any kind of good work. It may sound like God is stuck with us, that He's sadly resigned to working through such flawed people, but I don't think that is true. I get the sense God loves to work through weak, fearful, negligent, hateful, judgmental, doubting, prejudiced, perplexed, "prone to wander" people. Indeed, it seems to be the way He planned to do His work.

Consider these words from the Apostle Paul:

"But we have this treasure in jars of clay to show that this all-surpassing power is from God and not from us. We are hard pressed on every side, but not crushed; perplexed, but not in despair; persecuted, but not abandoned; struck down, but not destroyed." (2 Corinthians 4:7-9)

The "treasure" is the light of Jesus in us being displayed to others. It's the power and life of Jesus at work in us. So,

God does His good work through fragile clay jars, through people who are perplexed and pressed and knocked down. Why? It enables people to more clearly see the power and goodness of God. After all, we want people to be amazed by God and drawn to Him rather than to us. At least that's what we want in our best moments. And when I see God at work in someone as broken as I am, it helps to guard me from arrogance and self-righteousness and looking down on others. God's the hero, not me.

Further, God seems to do a good work even through our worst struggles and failures. On the heels of King David's horrific choices, he ends up penning one of the most passionate prayers of repentance ever recorded. Psalm 51 has helped an untold number of people navigate their hearts back to God, to find grace, and to turn from destructive behaviors. I'm one of that untold number. I've been stunned to discover that the sharing of my own struggles has moved many people to open up to trusted friends to find grace and healing and strength to change directions. Sometimes, it feels that God has done more good work through my "partly wrong" than my "partly right." I'll let God sort that out, but I can echo the words of the Apostle Paul, who affirmed:

"If I must boast, I will boast of the things that show my

weakness" and "...for when I am weak, then am I strong."
(2 Corinthians 11:30 and 12:10)

So, God does His good work through partly wrong people. It's not the plan I would've chosen, but I'm partly wrong, after all. There's a power to this plan. I, the broken, am able to clearly see that God did something I couldn't possibly have pulled off, which helps to keep me humble and God-dependent. At the same time, others are able to see clearly that it was God who worked, thus drawing them to Him and His ways. And oddly enough, being "partly wrong" allows God to do His work through me in a uniquely powerful way. I've learned that God has His own odd way of doing things...like that time he spoke to me through talk radio.

PARTLY WRONG

Chapter Six

***

WHAT'S WRONG WITH THE WORLD?

Trolling my van's radio dial for classic rock on a recent drive, I happened across two voices. It was talk radio. I immediately picked up the voice of a caller who spoke fluent Christianese. What was wrong with the world, at least for that hour's discussion purposes, was single moms whose families were supported by state money. Caller and host spoke with great passion and annoyance.

I winced as the radio host casually referenced "those

people." The caller quickly clarified that she was *not* one of "those people," that her six children had one father, who lived at home and worked. The caller and host agreed: We've got to do something about "those people." They discussed ideas, including requiring "those people" to attend church training. I was biting my tongue at this point.

It is sobering and disturbing how often we Christians paint "those people" as what's wrong with the world. We list off all the evidences of how dark things are, how deeply our world has fallen from the heart and ways of God, citing alarming statistics regarding abortions, suicides, AIDS, crime, addiction, murder, divorce, single parent families, etc. And those soul-filled statistics are deeply troubling. Something has gone wrong with our world.

So what has gone wrong? What or who is responsible? In my corner of Christianville, the answers come quickly, almost involuntarily: It's those people who kicked God out of the schools; it's those liberal media people and their agenda; it's those godless Hollywood producers; it's those pro-choice fanatics. It's those people who protest by taking a knee during the singing of the national anthem. It's those people.

Those people who are breaking the heart of God. Those people who are ruining our country. Those people are bringing the judgment of God on our world.

Decades ago, the London Times selected a variety of writers to submit an essay on the question: "What's wrong with the world?" Perhaps the most memorable essay was submitted by a controversial Christian writer, whose essay was composed of two words. "I am." He signed it, "Sincerely yours, G.K. Chesterton. (Philip Yancey, Soul Survivor: How My Faith Survived the Church, Random House, 2002, Kindle version, 991)

Chesterton—Christian, writer, speaker, apologist—spoke what's true of every partly wrong person. I'm what's wrong with the world. Wow. You don't hear that very often from Christians. Honestly, you don't hear that very often from anyone.

This rare admission is fundamentally true of all of us. Partly wrong, I'm what's wrong with the world. You're what's wrong with the world. We're what's wrong with the world. It's not just those people. It's all of us. We're all partly wrong. We all miss the mark of God's righteousness. We all wound and divide and grieve and offend.

Do you dare consider the possibility that you're a part of what's wrong with the world? Do I? We should...if I accurately understand the words of Jesus, who said:

"You are the light of the world. A town built on a hill cannot be hidden. Neither do people light a lamp and put it under a bowl. Instead they put it on its stand, and it gives light to everyone in the house. In the same way, let your light shine before others, that they may see your good deeds and glorify your Father in heaven. (Matthew 5:14-16)

Here's the funny thing about darkness. It only exists as the absence of light. You don't have a switch in your house to turn on the darkness. Darkness comes when you turn off or cover the light. So, if our world is dark, it begs the question: What happened to the light? How has the light been covered or veiled?

We need to ask ourselves some honest questions like: What if my judgmentalism is part of the darkness? What if my self-righteousness is what's wrong with the world? What if retreat into my own "safe" Christian subculture has enhanced the darkness? What if my arrogance has fostered greater darkness? What if yelling angry slogans and waving clever posters from across the street has contributed to the darkness? What if talking about "those people" on radio talk shows is what's wrong with the world? What if my contempt for judgmental Christians on talk radio is what's wrong with the world?

If I understand Jesus' words, partly wrong people must see how they're part of the problem and ask God to help them change and bring more light. We must pray: "God, help me see where I'm not living out the light. Help me see where I'm wrong and contributing to the darkness." When considering what's wrong with the world, partly wrong people must start with the person who greets them in the mirror each morning, as Michael Jackson memorably reminded us.

If we blame what's wrong with the world on "those people", we change neither them nor us. We both stay as wrong as we ever were. But when we humbly ask God to help change us, part of the world gets better and we're then in a better position to help others see where they may be part of the problem.

This is precisely what Jesus tells us to do: *"...first take the plank out of your own eye, and then you will see clearly to remove the speck from your brother's eye." (Matthew 7:5)*

Why don't we all look in the mirror, and start working on that plank. So, how do you identify the plank...or planks? You need outside help to see what you can't. The Bible psalmist prayed: *"But who can discern their own errors? Forgive my hidden faults." (Psalm 19:12)* A few years back, I began to pray and ask God to reveal flaws or planks in me that I can't see. That was a mistake, because that's one of those prayers God *always* seems to answer.

So, here is the annoying thing that God began to do. Someone would do something to me that was annoying, hurtful or hypocritical. Just as I began to stew about it, God would bring to mind some way in which I had done a similar thing. Or the exact same thing. That will shut down a pity party in a hurry. I thought God would run out of planks to show me. We have not had that problem yet. Even after that afternoon listening to talk radio, God began surfacing subtle "those people" attitudes that I myself entertained.

I dare you to pray the same prayer I prayed: "God, show me the planks." As you read the pages of the Bible and encounter stories of the broken choices of others, ask God: "Could I be doing that same thing?" Seek out a friend who loves you enough to be honest, and ask them about a flaw or sin of yours that needs attention. You may need to clarify that they point out just one for starters!

Operating from this posture of humble teachability, God will begin to show you ways in which you're what's wrong with the world. Don't be discouraged when He does, because no one is more eager to forgive and help you change those ways than He is.

While you're waiting for God to show you your plank, let me tell you about a plank God uncovered for me. It turns out that arguing is NOT a spiritual gift. I obviously disagree.

Chapter Seven

***

FACEBOOK WARS AND THE DEATH OF DIALOGUE

When I was in high school, I loved to debate. I'd been honing my craft for years, but my parents failed to appreciate my mad skills. They called it arguing. I disagreed, citing five obvious reasons they were wrong. Years later, Mom and Dad are still in denial....and therapy.

High school allowed me to take my skills from our home to the classroom, where I had a chance to participate in formal debate—an odd format that actually had rules. This debate involved two sides: a proposition and an opposition, affirmative and negative. Each side proposed its view in an opening statement, rebutted the views of the other in a second round, and summarized its position in a final statement. Even with these rules, I loved debate.

I loved debating for the same reason that I loved playing sports. I loved winning. Debate was all about winning; So was I. It was a perfect match. And I had some skills that lent themselves to winning debates. Economist Sandy Ikeda, describes such skills.

"Likewise, a good debater, because the object of debate is victory by any means short of violence, will zero in on her opponent's weakest argument, his most outrageous comment or slip of the tongue, and make it the centerpiece of a relentless attack in the hopes of hammering him to submission or making him look ridiculous in the eyes of any spectators. She will twist subtle argument into absurdity. Ad hominem, the straw man, and name-calling may be logical fallacies, but they're all part of the debater's arsenal, as are distraction and attributing false statements to an opponent.... Anyone who doesn't do such things is a bad debater." (Sandy Ikeda, *Discussion Vss. Debate*, fee.org, 2014)

Everything Mr. Ikeda listed...I was good at that. I could be pretty funny at times. I could think well on my feet. I had the gift of sarcasm. I possessed uncanny selective logic. I had a good eye for weaknesses and inconsistencies...in others. Did I mention my gift for sarcasm? I was good at winning debates.

I loved debates then. Not any more. I dislike presidential debates. I dislike newsroom debates. I especially dislike religious debates. You know why? Because they usually do more harm than good. Most debates don't help partly wrong people like me get more right. They're more likely to do the opposite. A debate feels like ignorance and arrogance just waiting to happen.

I don't like debates now for the very reason I loved them in high school. They're about winning. With debates, we use won/lost language. Surveys are taken after presidential debates. Polls are conducted after religious debates. Why? Well, you have to figure out who won! And consider the verbs used to describe the way of the winner. I've seen words like crushed, obliterated, owned, demolished, mopped the floor with, dominated. You rarely see words like learned, persuaded, challenged, encouraged, or taught. Debates are about winning, and if you can humiliate the other debater, even better.

On some Christian website, I recently saw a link to a video clip from the Stephen Colbert show where he hosts Bart Ehrman, an author whose recent book questioned whether Jesus is God. The caption read something like: "Watch this, and by the end you will be cheering." Anytime someone predicts what my reaction will be, I'm already skeptical. Uh...you don't know me. Well, I wasn't cheering at the end. Steaming, perhaps. Or growling. Not cheering.

You know why? Mr. Ehrman would make simple statements, only to be repeatedly interrupted by Colbert's mocking questions. This is, of course, Colbert's shtick, and the crowd loved it. Colbert sounded like me in my high school debate days. Poke fun at an inconsistency. Question the intelligence of the speaker. Win the crowd to your side with laughter. What was missing was any thoughtful dialogue on a question that really matters. There was nothing to help move Colbert and Ehrman and the audience any closer toward the heart of God.

I see this same harsh debating posture with growing frequency on Facebook and other online social networks. The discussion of any meaningful topic usually turns into a cafeteria fight with people lobbing barbs, accusations, names and labels rather than thoughtful ideas, helpful alternatives, and respectful affirmations. And none of us are any closer then to getting more right.

Debates often create an adversarial environment that discourages learning. When you attend or watch a debate, you usually lean toward one side or the other. You take a side. Put another way, there's someone you hope will "win." It's like going to a boxing match. You want "your guy" to knock the other guy out. Debates encourage taking sides. In a debate, you have an "opponent." Rather than seeing him and his supporters as people who could help me learn, I see them as combatants who're working against me. They're the enemy.

Debates are more about proving that I'm right than learning where I'm wrong. In fact, to ever admit in a debate that some part of your idea was wrong would result in an immediate "loss" of the debate. Think about that. In a debate, discovering and admitting you're wrong is considered a loss. Learning is actually losing. Growth is a casualty.

Another potential casualty is humility. Debates have a way of fostering arrogance. The central goal of a debate is to convince people that your claim or proposition is right. You must rebut any idea or fact that undermines your claims. You'll question every argument that suggests you could be wrong. Debate discourages any thinking that I may be wrong. Oh, and there's another problem. You can be wrong and "win" the debate. The post-debate poll names you the winner. The Facebook "likes" outnumber the critical comments. The applause for you overwhelms the thin claps for your opponent. It all affirms your confidence that you're right...even when you're wrong.

When debates are about winning, we all lose. Learning is lost. Humility is lost. Critical thinking is lost. Growth is lost. We need something better than debate. We need dialogue. By dialogue, I mean: thoughtful respectful discussions with others who can help us think through what we believe. We need respectful—even if sometimes heated—discussions that can help us to see where we may be wrong.

We need more dialogue and less debate. In debate, we're trying to prove or expose the other person as wrong. In dialogue, we're discussing things together to help clarify the truth. Debate starts with the belief that I'm right and you're wrong. Dialogue start with the belief that we both have some things right and some things wrong, and we need discussion to figure out what's right.

I've come down hard on debate in order to highlight some of its lurking dangers, but I'm not looking to end all debate. The one thing I still love about debate is that people who disagree are talking to each other. That's huge, and I've experienced debates that felt more like a conversation than a battle. If partly wrong people are ever to learn where they're wrong, they must seek thoughtful, respectful dialogue with people who think differently. Let's debate with a posture of dialogue. When that happens, everyone wins.

So, let's invite those who disagree with us into dialogue. Few people have done this better than Martin Luther King, Jr. If you went right now and read his "Letter from a Birmingham Jail," to the white Birmingham clergy, you'd learn more about dialogue with disagree-ers than anything I've written in this chapter. I'll simply quote one of the earliest lines in his letter, along with the last:

"But since I feel that you are men of genuine good will and your criticisms are sincerely set forth, I would like to answer your statement in what I hope will be patient and reasonable terms...If I have said anything in this letter that is an understatement of the truth and is indicative of an unreasonable impatience, I beg you to forgive me. If I have said anything in this letter that is an overstatement of the truth and is indicative of my having a patience that makes me patient with anything less than brotherhood, I beg God to forgive me." (*The Atlantic Monthly,* August, 1963: *The Negro Is Your Brother*, Vol. 212, No. 2, pgs. 78-88)

If you've read the letter, you know that he voiced strong and discomforting convictions while addressing the questions of his critics. So why bookend those comments with such gracious and respectful words? A friend once heard Dr. Robert Smith Jr. say this about Dr. King: "He wasn't about winning; He was about reconciliation." When the goal of our debates is winning, we'll lose the things that matter most. When we invite and encourage dialogue, we all win and get a bit closer to right.

Another kind of dialogue is reading a book. If you like books...or games...you may enjoy my trivia question in the next chapter.

Chapter Eight

***

I'VE NOTHING TO LEARN FROM YOU

I love to read. I can't remember when I didn't. Mom and Dad would tuck me into bed as a kid, but after they left, I would sneak out a flashlight so I could finish reading a book. A granddaughter of mine does the same (don't tell her parents), and I could not be more proud. I love books, words, reading, and word games, so you must forgive me for asking you a trivia question about books. The following books all have something significant in common. What do you think it is?

Origin of Species, by Charles Darwin

Uncle Tom's Cabin, by Harriet Beecher Stowe

Animal Farm, by George Orwell

To Kill a Mockingbird, by Harper Lee

Age of Reason, by Thomas Paine

Mein Kampf, by Adolph Hitler

Bury My Heart at Wounded Knee, by Dee Brown

The Kingdom of God is Within You, by Leo Tolstoy

Satanic Verses, by Salmon Rushdie

So, what ties all these books together?

They are all books that have been banned, censored or prohibited from distribution by some organization, government or board.

But why? Why are books censored? The history of "banned" books is fascinating. Many books have been banned because they're considered obscene. Other books have been banned because they're seen to encourage illegal or immoral activity. Books have been banned because they were considered dangerous—for instance, books that describe how to make bombs. Books have been banned in some countries because they described something unflattering about that country or its government. Books have been banned because they have hateful or controversial words like the "n-word," for instance. "Black Beauty" (yes, the book about the horse) was actually banned in Apartheid South Africa in 1955 because it had the word "black" in its title! (www.banned-books.org.uk/all)

But the books listed above have been banned for a different reason. They were banned because they expressed ideas or a telling of history considered dangerous or wrong or heretical. The books contained ideas that some felt would lead readers into erroneous ideas or behavior. We can't have you reading that!

Growing up in churchworld, I knew something about censorship. I don't remember specific "banned book" lists, though I'm sure there were some in our circles. Our censorship sounded more like this: "You don't need to be reading books by (that author)." "You should avoid visiting churches from (that denomination)." "It wouldn't be wise to go to a conference sponsored by (that organization)." "Don't listen to material from (that teacher)." Fill in your own blanks, but I've heard names like Anthony Campolo, Pentecostals, Billy Graham, Catholics, Rob Bell, Muslims, Joel Osteen.

So, why should you close your eyes and ears to the ideas of these people? Well, you could be led astray. Those people and their ideas could lead you to compromise. We can't have you hearing or entertaining wrong and dangerous ideas.

The banning was rarely tied to an actual printed out list, but you had a pretty good sense of which groups and authors and ideas and viewpoints were "off limits." A name might show up in a sermon...or a comment...or an article. It was an understood, "organic" censorship.

Of course, this subtle censorship is not limited to churches or religious groups. It occurs in educational circles, scientific societies, businesses, and other organizations.

Brian Martin describes some forms of scientific censorship:

"A common method of stopping the message is peer review and editorial control. To obtain scientific credibility, a viewpoint needs to be published in the scientific literature, preferably in a prestigious journal. In many fields, there is widespread consensus about what is considered to be correct. This can be called a 'paradigm,' which is a dominant way of thinking about the world and carrying out research within a field...The normal operation of peer review does not seem to be a form of censorship, since it is presented as a form of quality control. However, assessments of quality cannot be separated from assessments of what are valid questions and what are valid ways to carry out research. Challenges to the current paradigm are seldom seen as valid." (Brian Martin, *Censorship: A World Encyclopedia*, Volume 4, edited by Derek Jones (London: Fitzroy Dearborn, 2001), pp. 2167-2170.)

I think of churches when I read "there is widespread consensus about what is considered to be correct" and "challenges to the current paradigm are seldom seen as valid." In scienceworld, an idea or paradigm that goes against the "widespread consensus" can effectively be censored by peer review and other indirect methods. Widespread consensus becomes the basis for censorship. In other words, there are certain ideas or beliefs so entrenched that you can't propose—or even discuss—an alternative idea. Why? We already know the truth. We don't want others to be led astray. Those people and their ideas could compromise long held ideas. We can't have our people hearing or entertaining wrong and dangerous ideas.

Uh, sounds like some thinking I heard growing up in

church.

And it's only recently that I realized just how arrogant and dangerous that thinking in our churches was, and is. For years I chafed at such thinking and challenged it, but only recently did I feel the full weight of its deep arrogance. Does that word seem too strong? For me, it may not be strong enough.

When we told people not to read other authors, not to listen to other teachers, not to go to other churches, we were effectively saying, "We're absolutely right about everything. There's nothing we can possibly be wrong about. There's no place where our ideas and viewpoints need correction. If anyone disagrees with us on anything, they're wrong." To believe anything different than we did made one wrong, so anyone who taught anything different than we did would be leading you astray.

There's nothing more arrogant than saying "we're right on everything" or "we can't possibly be wrong." Nothing's more arrogant—or foolish—because...well, because we're all partly wrong. Partly wrong on some small things. Partly wrong on some big things. And when we forbid people to read or hear or consider different ideas, we're robbing ourselves of the chance to see places where we may be wrong, places where we need to shift our thinking, ideas we need to reconsider, things for which we should repent. When we ourselves refuse to read, much less consider, different ideas, we've no way of seeing places where we're wrong. Thinking we're right about everything, and avoiding any counter ideas, we more deeply entrench our wrong ideas.

But, Roger, isn't there a place for discouraging reading sometimes? Some things might not be age-appropriate for a child. And for anyone, some material might be obscene or hateful or terror-based. I hear you. There's a place for discernment, but there's a danger to censorship that attempts to silence the voice of anyone who disagrees with me. Such censorship kills learning and petrifies wrong ideas, often with serious consequences.

Consider what happened 2000 years ago when Jesus began teaching the ways of God. Some of His ideas ran directly counter to the "widespread consensus" of the religion of the day. So, religious teachers and leaders stalked him, trying to expose his falsehoods. They challenged him. They threatened him. They mocked him. They blacklisted him or people who supported him. One formerly blind man who praised Jesus was put out of the synagogue.

Certain they couldn't be wrong, these Jewish leaders censored and shut themselves off to the truth that could reconcile them to the God they thought they knew perfectly.

But this wasn't the story of everyone who heard the message about Jesus. When Paul (the Jew who came to believe the message he once violently censored) took the message about Jesus to the city of Berea, their response was striking:

"Now the Berean Jews were of more noble character than those in Thessalonica, for they received the message with great eagerness and examined the Scriptures every day to see if what Paul said was true." (Acts 17:11)

What these Berean Jews did here is actually remarkable. You see, this message of Paul went against the core religious paradigm these Jews had embraced their entire lives. His message was controversial, uncomfortable, even offensive. But they listened anyway. They wrestled with the ideas. They checked out the Scriptures to see whether these new ideas were consistent, considering the possibility that their understanding of the Scriptures might've been wrong. In the process, many of them concluded they'd been wrong on some key ideas, and they shifted. They learned. They grew. They moved closer to the heart of God. But it only happened because they refused to censor someone with a different paradigm.

One of the greatest gifts I received from my parents was the encouragement to read and listen broadly. Mom and Dad were teachers and not censors. I'm sure that there were authors and poets and songwriters about which they had significant concerns, but they encouraged listening with a discerning and examining ear. They chose scholarship over censorship. This was an invaluable grace, without which this book could never have been written.

Censorship will invariably have the effect of blinding us to ideas of ours which are wrong. But sometimes, that's exactly what we want. Sometimes we censor ideas or authors or movements because we don't want them to be right. It's not simply an arrogant belief that we can't be wrong. Sometimes we don't care if we're wrong.

In 1972, Luther Ingram sang the soulful song: "I don't want to be right." (Songwriters: Homer Banks, Carl Hampton, Raymond Jackson, Stax Records) If loving a particular girl was wrong, he declared, "I don't want to be right." The words resonated deeply with people, and it was at or near the top of R&B charts for several weeks that year. Lyrics like those would typically be frowned on in churchworld, but surely we have felt that same tension.

If segregating church services is wrong, I don't want to be right.
If cutting state benefits for the poor is wrong, I don't want to be right.
If sleeping with my girlfriend is wrong, I don't want to be right.
If divorcing my wife is wrong, I don't want to be right.
If hating ISIS terrorists is wrong, I don't want to be right.
If choosing abortion is wrong, I don't want to be right.
If deporting desperate immigrants is wrong, I don't want to be right.

Of course, this is not limited to churchworld. It's found in science world, business world, philosophy world. I appreciate the honesty of philosopher Thomas Nagel, who writes:

"I want atheism to be true and am made uneasy by the fact that some of the most intelligent and well-informed people I know are religious believers. It isn't just that I don't believe in God and, naturally, hope that I'm right in my belief. It's that I hope there is no God! I don't want there to be a God; I don't want the universe to be like that." (The Last Word by Thomas Nagel, Oxford University Press: 1997, pp. 130-131)

None of us escape this tension. I know I don't. There are ideas or claims that I definitely don't want to be true. However, it's both foolish and dangerous to refuse to read or listen to ideas I dislike or fear. In order to learn where I'm wrong, I must be willing to hear out ideas I think are wrong.

Brian Martin makes a plea to his friends in the scientific community, but it's a great word for all of us in the church community: "...there are plenty of examples of theories, such as continental drift, that were once treated as outlandish and later became accepted wisdom. However, the key thing is not whether a viewpoint is ultimately judged to be correct, but rather whether it is given a fair hearing, even if it turns out to be wrong." (Brian Martin, pp. 2167-2170)

It's vital that we partly wrong people give a fair hearing to ideas that run counter to our own. Just like the community of Jews in Berea, we should read, listen to, and wrestle with, controversial ideas in order to discern where we may be wrong. The idea we least want to hear may be what we most need to hear.

Remember that before you read the next chapter: What Sodom Got Wrong.

Chapter Nine

***

WHAT SODOM GOT WRONG

"At least I'm not an axe-murderer."

This is a colorful way of saying, "I've got issues, but not like others do," or "Sure, I'm wrong on some things--small things--but I'm not wrong on the big things. I struggle with sin, but not with the serious stuff." This thinking is founded on one critical assumption: some wrongs or sins are worse than others—more serious, more offensive, more harmful, more evil, more disturbing to God.

I used to believe that. It was obvious...that is, until God took me on an uncomfortable journey through the Bible that challenged my assumptions and exposed my heart. I'd like to take you on that same journey--partly because I don't want to be uncomfortable all by myself, but mostly because the Word of God did a world of good in my heart.

I want to start the journey with an exercise that will involve some reflection on your part. Humor me. Below is a list of behaviors and choices that various people would label as sin, something they believe God identifies as wrong. Read slowly through the list and reflect on these questions: Do some of these feel "worse" or more serious than others? Do some feel wrong at all? Or do you read through these and have the feeling that they're all the same?

Telling a lie
Underpaying a worker
Stirring up trouble in relationships
Disobeying a parent
Coveting something that belongs to someone else
Arrogance
Ignoring the needs of the poor
Rape

Thinking you're superior to another person

Overindulgence

Murder

Disregarding God

Withholding forgiveness from someone

Adultery

Divorce

Not caring for the needs of immigrants

Adultery

Religious hypocrisy

Gossip

Homosexual relationship

Withholding mercy

Loving something or someone more than God

Are there some things on this list that you believe are more serious or evil than others? Are there some things on this list that God sees as especially evil? If so, take a moment in your mind to identify which ones those might be. You may even want to pencil them down somewhere.

Now, we're in a position to see how accurate we are in assessing evil. You see, in the Bible, you will occasionally see the word "abomination" or "detestable" or the phrase "God hates" this behavior. In a few places, there's actually a listing of such behaviors. I thought it might be helpful for us to consider three such lists to help us assess our own lists. Before we check out the first list, go ahead and pull out your "serious sin" list, and let's see how it compares:

"There are six things the Lord hates, seven that are detestable (or "abomination," in the KJV) to him: haughty eyes, a lying tongue, hands that shed innocent blood, a heart that devises wicked schemes, feet that are quick to rush into evil, a false witness who pours out lies and a person who stirs up conflict in the community." (Proverbs 6:16-19)

O.K., so the first on the list is haughty eyes, which is seeing yourself as better than others. God says that is detestable. Telling a lie. Detestable. Murder. Detestable. Scheming evil. Detestable. Quick to do wrong. Detestable. Lying about someone else. Detestable. Stirring up trouble in a family or community. Detestable.

I don't know about you, but the only thing on the list I would have labeled as detestable is murder. How is it that I never think of lying as detestable or an abomination? Or looking at others like I am superior to them? Could it be because I lie and look down at others often but have never murdered someone? Those murderers do detestable things, but not me!

Here's what gives me pause. I've done six of the seven things on this "detestable" list, but I only see one as detestable...the one thing I haven't done. Is that a remarkable coincidence or remarkable hypocrisy? Hmmm. Maybe I just got unlucky on this list. Let's try another one.

There's another "serious" list in the Bible, recorded in Romans, chapter 1. The Apostle Paul introduces this list with these words: "The wrath of God is being revealed from heaven against all the godlessness and wickedness of people, who..." He lists all kinds of things, but I will take us partway down the list to this section, which reads:

"In the same way the men also abandoned natural relations with women and were inflamed with lust for one another. Men committed shameful acts with other men, and received in themselves the due penalty for their error. Furthermore, just as they did not think it worthwhile to retain the knowledge of God, so God gave them over to a depraved mind, so that they do what ought not to be done. They have become filled with every kind of wickedness, evil, greed and depravity. They are full of envy, murder, strife, deceit and malice. They are gossips, slanderers, God-haters, insolent, arrogant and boastful; they invent ways of doing evil; they disobey their

parents; 31 they have no understanding, no fidelity, no love, no mercy." (Romans 1:27-31)

Paul references same-sex sexual intimacy in this list. Now I know some people would absolutely put this on their "wickedness" or "abomination" list. But in this exact same passage, the Bible lists wicked behaviors like "gossip, withholding mercy, greed, envy, and disobeying parents." Wow. I don't know about you, but none of those made my "really wicked" list. How convenient, particularly since I have been greedy, unmerciful, disobedient to parents, envious, etc. Surely, that is just another coincidence, right!? There's no way I would downplay the seriousness of my own sins and demonize the sins I don't commit. Right? By the way, how are you doing with your list?

So, God led me to one more "list" check. The Bible recounts the sobering judgment of God against an ancient city called Sodom. God literally destroyed the entire city and virtually every person in it. This still staggers and disturbs me. A city had become so corrupt and so dangerous that God would think it best to eliminate that city. What could they've possibly done to bring this kind of judgment on them? Well, the prophet Ezekiel gives us a list of their sins.

"Now this was the sin of your sister Sodom: She and her daughters were arrogant, overfed and unconcerned; they did not help the poor and needy. 50 They were haughty and did detestable things before me. Therefore I did away with them as you have seen. 51 Samaria did not commit half the sins you did. You have done more detestable things than they, and have made your sisters seem righteous by all these things you have done." (Ezekiel 16:49-51)

Here's a basic paraphrase of the list. The people of Sodom thought they were right about everything and superior to others. They were gluttons, obsessed with themselves. They were apathetic and didn't help the poor and needy. They were snobbish and did detestable things. And while Ezekiel did not specify the "detestable" things, some have identified that as their homosexual lifestyle and practices.

Now, I grew up in the church, and we tended to rank sins, and I assure you that homosexuality was near the top of the "abomination" list. In fact, it was the only sin of Sodom that I ever heard mentioned. The ONLY one. When it came to over-indulgence and not helping the poor and needy—I'm not even sure they even made our "sin" list, much less a "worthy of fiery judgment" list. Never in all my church life do I recall hearing that arrogance or materialism or failure to care for the poor were the reason for God's judgment of Sodom.

Oh, and did you catch what God said through the prophet to His chosen people, Israel—the "people of God?" I'll paraphrase: "Your sins are far worse than Sodom's sins. Your sins make the people of Sodom look like Mother Teresa." While I don't remember Israel being rebuked by God for their homosexuality, they're repeatedly chastised by God for arrogance, disregarding God, and neglecting the poor. Among so many church voices I hear today, there's no hint that we—the non-gay Christians—could possibly be violating shalom or disobeying God more than gays. If I understand the words of the prophet, our hypocrisy and arrogance may well be the primary source of God's greatest judgment. After all, it does appear that the "first ever" sin in the universe--and source of every other sin--was the arrogance of Satan. It seems that a primary manifestation of arrogance could be castigating the wrongs of others while downplaying our own wrongs or dismissing them altogether.

As God took me down this journey, He exposed my heart, and indicted my own evil. I had to throw away my "really bad sins" list. Maybe you fared better than I did.

Are some sins worse than others? I can't answer that question with any certainty, but I don't think you and I have any business trying to make that call, and here's why. Our answers lead to more sin, more wrongs, and more violation of God's shalom. Invariably, we're selective and hypocritical. When assessing the sins of others as "worse," we find it easier to judge them and harder to love them. Further, we almost always trivialize our own sins and wrongs, minimizing our own desperate need for grace and forgiveness. Attempting to rank sin increases our own. It moves us further from God's heart rather than closer. It gets us more wrong than right.

Every sin is a violation of shalom and moves us further from God's heart. Every sin is evil. Our greatest need is to acknowledge our own sin and come back home to the Father who longs to forgive our every sin, even the hypocrisy and arrogance of ranking everyone else's sins. Our humble calling is to tell other sinners that God offers us all a pardon and a way home, made possible by Jesus.

On the way home to the Father's house, God wants us to begin doing life in a church community, and that's where things can get messy.

Chapter Ten

***

THE PERFECT CHURCH

Jesus once said: *"where two or three gather in my name, there am I with them."* (Matthew 18:20, NIV) [Cue the strumming of harps.] Jesus' words are a beautiful reality, but here's another reality. Where two or three gather in Jesus' name, they're still partly wrong. When partly wrong people gather together as a church, their wrongs don't cancel each other out. Sometimes, the partly wrongs multiply. Churches—like people, and because they are made up of people—are partly wrong.

Wrong beliefs. Wrong motives. Wrong methods. Wrong attitudes.

I was part of a church with a strong sense of mission to love a neglected and forgotten neighborhood. Following that lead, we began meeting in the community center in an area that people in passing cars would call "the projects." From the parking lot of our community center, you could see the rows and rows of dingy red brick buildings surrounded by sagging clotheslines and green plastic trash cans.

One Sunday morning, I stood in that parking lot and watched as a trickle of vans and buses with faded church names edged their way among the brick buildings, providing rides for residents to church buildings far away. And I thought to myself: "those churches come into our neighborhood to bring people out, but we actually have church right here in their neighborhood." I was immediately seized by the arrogance and judgmentalism of my thoughts. I proved anew the reality of the partly wrong church. Partly wrong attitudes. Partly wrong practices. Partly wrong ideas.

Some churches meet in "the projects," and some meet in

the suburbs. Some churches send people out to knock on
doors, and some go out and wash people's cars. Some
churches sing quiet, classical hymns carried along by organ
bellows, and some churches make a joyful noise with
guitars and drums. Some churches invite people to the
altar to receive the bread and the cup of the Lord's Table,
and some churches take the bread and cup to people where
they sit. Some churches meet weekly on Sundays, some
weekly on Saturdays, and some daily in homes. Church
practices are different.

Church beliefs are different. Some churches believe that
God enables people to do miraculous things—like healing
sick people—while other churches don't. Some churches
believe that people enter God's kingdom by their choice,
and some churches believe people enter by God's choice.
Some churches believe that women can be pastors, and
some believe that role is only for men. Some churches
believe you shouldn't drink alcoholic beverages, and others
believe you may drink in moderation. The list of things
churches disagree about feels unending.

Does that concern you? Well, for the longest time, it
bothered me. I thought: "If the Holy Spirit is at work in all
believers and all churches, wouldn't they all believe the
same things? Wouldn't they agree on everything?

Wouldn't God simply show all of us exactly what's right?

My question made sense, but it didn't account for growth and learning and interdependence—core to God's plan for the world. My assumption would require Him to give all of us instantaneous perfect knowledge. That sounds awesome, but it isn't God's plan. Instead He says through the Apostle Peter:

"But grow in the grace and knowledge of our Lord and Savior Jesus Christ. To him be glory both now and forever! Amen. (2 Peter 3:18)

Every church has the need to grow in the grace and knowledge of Jesus. And how do we grow? In community with God and other Christians. No single church or denomination has everything right. There's no church that doesn't need to keep growing and re-evaluating and learning. There's no church that does not need other churches. There's no such thing as the perfect church. So pastors should stop striving to be the perfect church, people should stop looking for the perfect church, and churches should stop acting like they *are* the perfect church..

Not long ago, I heard a young pastor talk about wanting to

help build a "New Testament" church. I smiled. It took me back three decades to when I was planning to launch a new church in a quaint corner of Massachusetts. I too used that term "New Testament" church. I'd actually read A New Testament Blueprint for the Church, a helpful book by John Moore and Kenneth Neff.

I realize now what I was looking for in the "New Testament" church was the perfect church—that church that was doing everything right, just like the very first church described in the book of Acts. With the best of motive, I wanted to build a church that got it all right. It was a misguided quest, now comical to me, since the New Testament church was a mess, marred by racism, lying, and pride. Further, there wasn't this single template for the practice of every church in the New Testament.

My quest for the perfect church led me through a steady stream of books and conferences, each offering another promise of the church that finally got things right. The options were endless. We could be the purpose-driven church, the seeker-sensitive church, the missional community church, the home church, the liturgical church, the charismatic church, the congregational-led church, the fivefold gifts church, the lifestyle evangelism church, the simple church, the vision-driven church, the elder-led

church, the multi-ethnic church, the homogeneous church,
the victorious life church, the community development
church, the full gospel church, the reformed church...
(pause for air).

To the pastors reading my words. Relax. Seek God as to
how to best lead your church. Read books and go to
conferences and get counsel from others, but stop trying to
get your church just right. The "just right" church does not
exist. You're always going to pastor a church that is partly
wrong. I'm not advocating complacency or laziness. I'm
advocating trust in a God who has only ever used partly
wrong pastors and partly wrong churches, including the
famed "New Testament" church. We must trust that God is
guiding us and also that He's redeeming and salvaging
what we're getting wrong.

It follows that the rest of us Jesus-followers can stop
looking for the perfect church. Someone has wryly
advised: If you ever find the perfect church, for heaven's
sake, don't join it because you'll ruin it. The search for the
perfect church is an impossible quest that'll leave in its
wake a discarded stream of partly wrong churches that
needed you as much as you needed them.

I'm not saying there's never a healthy reason for leaving

one church to move to another. But finding the perfect church isn't a healthy reason. For one, it's not possible. And second, the "perfect church" is often code for "church just the way I like it." Since you're partly wrong, the last thing you need is "church just the way you like it." You and I need to be stretched and disturbed and challenged to think differently. We need to persistently work through problems and misunderstandings and inconsistencies. We need to hang together to help each other become a bit less wrong.

And speaking of hanging together, church members and communities need to do more of that as well. Maybe instead of people leaving churches trying to find a better church, they could stay and help their church get better. Perhaps churches could be spending more time together helping each other become better churches.

Just as partly wrong people need other partly wrong people to help them become more like Jesus, partly wrong church communities need other partly wrong church communities to help them become more like the kingdom of heaven. Churches and denominations need each other.

I love watching how various streams of the Christian church balance and challenge and complement each other.

I love the deep faith in God that the Charismatics splash on God's church mural. I love the Catholic's deep respect for God, the reformed reverence for God's holiness, the activism of the Methodists, the simplicity of the Quakers, the evangelistic fervor of the Baptists, the worship of the Anglicans, and the Adventist's love for God's Word.

I wish I'd recognized the beauty and wisdom of the larger church much earlier. The church denomination in which I grew up, for all of its graces, viewed other denominations, at best, with suspicion, and at worst with outright condemnation. Worship with Charismatics was discouraged, and it was questionable whether Catholics were Christians at all. Ours was a posture of isolation. The isolation was meant to keep us from compromise. What it actually kept us from was balance. From growth. From community.

I recall the first time I had lunch with a Charismatic pastor. He exuded a love for God, and the stories from his church sounded an awful lot like the stories from my Baptist Church. I discovered that we were a lot more similar than different. I would learn, further, that there were verses in the Bible that I'd only seen from one angle. I'd things to learn from my Charismatic brother. I've had similar stretching and growth talking and worshiping with

Episcopalian, Church of Christ, Catholic and Seventh Day Adventist friends.

I'm closer to the heart of God for these interactions. Time with others has surfaced the misconceptions, blind spots, and places where I was missing something of the heart of God. I'm still partly wrong, of course, but the broader Christian church has helped me to grow far more than I would've had I remained in my Baptist incubator.

There's no perfect church. Every church has some flawed practices and ideas and attitudes.

If I could go back and talk to my 29-year old self preparing to start a church, I'd tell him: "Roger, you can't build the perfect church, but if you'll work and worship and talk with Christians from different churches, you'll get the next best thing: The learning church."

And if I could talk to my 29-year old self, I would also tell him, "you're more dangerous than you think you are, and I'm not talking about your golf swing."

Chapter Eleven

***

AMERICA'S MOST DANGEROUS PERSON

In 2009, the Sydney Opera and the Ethics Centre co-founded an annual event, "The Festival of Dangerous Ideas," which would continue on until 2016. The goal was to bring people together to discuss and debate important issues. Below is a listing of some of the ideas that were "presented" over the years.

Religion poisons everything.

Without God we are nothing.

Ecstacy is no more dangerous than horse-riding.

All women are sluts.

Israel is an Apartheid state.

The devil is real.

A fetus is not a person.

Some people are more equal than others.

A killer can be a good neighbor.

The rise of women has turned men into boys.

There is no war on drugs.

Did any of those ideas strike you as dangerous? I thought so. I'm guessing that some of those ideas got you fired up a bit. Ideas will do that, because ideas matter. Figuring out which of them are dangerous is challenging but important.

I recently saw a website article labeling Professor and Minister Tony Campolo as a "dangerous" man. Why was he considered dangerous? His dangerous ideas. He embraces and teaches and publishes wrong ideas. The writer was emphatic: That man and his ideas are a danger to people everywhere. I've seen similar warnings issued about Evangelist Billy Graham and Host Oprah Winfrey and Pastor Rick Warren and President Donald Trump. There are websites and organizations whose basic mission is identifying dangerous people and warning everyone else.

Identifying dangerous ideas is important.

Identifying dangerous people is dangerous.

When Jesus walked the earth, there were similar groups
on patrol for dangerous people. The Pharisees and Chief
Priests championed this role. Trolling public venues and
synagogue meetings and private conversations, they
listened carefully for dangerous people with dangerous
ideas. Jesus soon got their attention. It wasn't just one
idea or one claim or one teaching. He was a factory of
wrong ideas. They began regularly to challenge his claims
in public, but to no avail. People were taking his ideas
quite seriously. Lots of people. And this made him
especially dangerous. People were embracing his ideas. He
was swaying public opinion. They ultimately identified
him as the most dangerous person in their country. How
do I know? Well, listen in on a conversation they had
about him:

*"If we let him go on like this, everyone will believe in him,
and then the Romans will come and take away both our
temple and our nation." (John 11:48)*

What are they saying? If people continue to believe his

teachings, then our nation will cease to exist. Uh...that's pretty serious. You can't get much more dangerous than that. And so it's no surprise what they concluded at the end of their meeting.

"So from that day on they plotted to take his life." (John 11:53)

They essentially labeled him public enemy number one— the most dangerous man in Israel. He was so dangerous that he needed to be taken out.

Identifying dangerous people is dangerous.

It appears that they never considered the possibility that they themselves might be dangerous. Jesus had suggested this very thing. On one occasion, he called them "blind leaders of the blind." Blind people guiding blind people is dangerous. The problem of course is that they were blind to their own danger. They couldn't envision that they might be wrong.

Now here's where they were right. Wrong ideas can be very serious. When we encounter a dangerously wrong idea, we should urge a change in thinking. My meteorologist son and his colleagues do this all the time.

It is NOT safe to take shelter under a tree during a lightning storm. Do NOT attempt to drive your car through a flooded street. It's healthy to identify and challenge dangerous ideas.

The prophets and apostles in the Bible called out false ideas. The Pharisees should've been on the lookout for dangerous ideas. I don't believe that the Pharisees and Chief Priests were sinister, power-grabbing, hateful people. I think many genuinely wanted to stand for right and guard the truth. They didn't seem to seriously consider, however, that their ideas might be dangerous. They dismissed the possibility that they may be blind.

Are we really any different today? I've never read anyone who identified himself or herself as the "most dangerous person in America." I can't think of anyone who "outed" himself as a heretic. I am trying to think of anyone I've read or listened to who ever identified his own ideas as dangerous. It's always someone else.

Hmm.

Because here's the truth: Every single one of us is dangerous. By that I mean we have flawed, mistaken ideas that we're passing on to others. Of course Campolo and

Graham and Warren and Winfrey and Trump are dangerous; we all are, because we all have flawed ideas.

So I have a concern when we move from labeling dangerous ideas to labeling dangerous people. It subtly reinforces a belief that I'm not dangerous. But I am, and so are you. We all need help from others to identify our own wrong, dangerous ideas. When we've stamped "dangerous" on someone's forehead, we'll close ourselves off to anything else they have to say. That's exactly what happened with the Pharisees and Jesus. Jesus was the dangerous one, so they ignored his words and warned everyone else to reject Him. In the process, they became the most dangerous people in Israel, calling their people to ignore God Himself.

Here's a word from Jesus they should have paid close attention to:

"Why do you look at the speck of sawdust in your brother's eye and pay no attention to the plank in your own eye? How can you say to your brother, 'Let me take the speck out of your eye,' when all the time there is a plank in your own eye? You hypocrite, first take the plank out of your own eye, and then you will see clearly to remove the speck from your brother's eye." (Matthew

7:3-5)

Jesus doesn't discourage helping others with their dangerous ideas. He does, however, raise the uncomfortable possibility that we may have an even more dangerous idea. After all, a plank in your eye is more dangerous than a speck of sawdust. More dangerous still is the failure or refusal to see your own plank.

If you don't believe that you could be dangerous, you are.

And you're also a monster. Sort of. Well, not in the way you might be thinking. Or maybe it *is* the way you're thinking. Never mind. I'll clear it up in the next chapter.

PARTLY WRONG

Chapter Twelve

***

MONSTERS LIKE ME

The blogger I was reading was blunt: "Someone needs to put a baseball bat up this punk's ass." Other online commenters talked about the "little shit." So who's the punk?

On January 28, 2015, on the Stanford University campus, two Swedish international students discovered a man assaulting a woman who appeared to be unconscious. When they confronted him, the 19-year old fled the scene, only to be chased down by the two students and held until police could arrive. The restrained student, Stanford swimmer and Olympic hopeful Brock Turner, would later be indicted on charges of rape, attempted rape and felony sexual assault. He would eventually be convicted of attempted rape and sexual assault.

His father, Dan Turner, pled with the court for leniency, writing that a long sentence would be "a steep price to pay for 20 minutes of action out of his 20 years of life." (*Washington Post*, June 6, 2016) When his words were made public, many were furious. He'd later call it an "unfortunate choice of words," noting that he was simply contrasting 20 years and 20 minutes. Tragically, the entire letter downplayed the gravity of the assault.

The assaulted woman wrote a remarkable and poignant response to her attacker, capturing the breadth of damage inflicted on her body, soul, and life. Her heart-wrenching words created an indelible image of the horror and gravitas of a sexual assault. A judge ultimately sentenced Brock Turner to 6 months confinement in jail to be followed by three years of probation and permanent registration as a sex offender.

Almost everything about this story pained me. The evil

assault. The irremovable damage to this woman. The downplaying of the attack. The way the woman was questioned by lawyers. The "slap on the wrist" sentence. And the bloggers calling him "punk" and "little shit."

Whoa, Roger. You weren't infuriated by what Brock Turner did? Don't you think his actions were evil? You'd rather we call him "outstanding swimmer?" You don't think he's a punk? A monster? A little shit?

Those are loaded questions. What he did is inexcusable, but I wonder if we aren't on dangerous ground when we start attaching sinister labels to other partly wrong people. Monsters. Animals. Piece of Trash. Little Shit. Garbage. Slut. When I hear those labels, I can't get a particular word from Jesus out of my mind.

One morning, Jesus was preparing to teach, when He had a highly unusual interruption. Here's the Bible's account.

"At dawn he appeared again in the temple courts, where all the people gathered around him, and he sat down to teach them. The teachers of the law and the Pharisees brought in a woman caught in adultery. They made her stand before the group and said to Jesus, 'Teacher, this woman was caught in the act of adultery. In the Law

Moses commanded us to stone such women. Now what do you say?' They were using this question as a trap, in order to have a basis for accusing him." (John 8:2-6)

In all my years of teaching, I've never had an interruption like this. A group of men—religious leaders—walk in, parading a frightened embarrassed woman, and they force her to stand up in front of everyone. They announce that she's been caught in the act of committing adultery. Pause to envision this moment. Take a look at the woman. Take a look at the men who brought her in. Let the scene settle into your spirit.

***

The picture is deeply troubling. How could religious leaders get to a place where they were so hard-hearted, cruel and harsh? The answer is discomforting. You see, adultery was a "monster" sin in that culture and time. People like that shouldn't even live, they thought. You know that we Americans have our own "monster" sins, don't you? They're easy to identify: Child molestation, rape, child porn, sexual assault, spouse abuse. Listen to the language we use about "those people." Animal. Piece of trash. Low life. Deviant. Pile of shit. Monster.

So, when you've given people a label like "monster" or "deviant" or "piece of trash," what happens? You treat them like trash. You throw them up in front of a crowd and talk about them like they aren't really even people. You might not even care whether they live or die.

I vaguely recall a popular crime show episode where a teen girl had been assaulted by a male camp worker. Years later, she unexpectedly encounters this person and ends up killing him. When the agents gradually piece together the whole history of the guy who was killed, they decide to "look the other way." Why? Because monsters aren't seen as real people anymore. Laws about human dignity and justice and due process don't apply to animals and monsters. They deserve whatever they get.

So, there's no shock to me that this woman is paraded around like a piece of trash to be mocked and abused. Honestly, we do the same thing in different ways. We talk about and blog about "monsters" in ways we don't with other people. We wish a special place in hell for "those kinds." And I believe there's a word God wants to speak to us through Jesus here.

Jesus absorbs the scene. The woman. The men. The brokenness of it all. Then He slowly goes down to his knees. What's He doing? Is He going to pray? Maybe. No, wait. He's using his fingers to write something on the dusty ground. I wonder what He's writing? Annoyed, the men continue to pepper him with questions about how to treat this...this...deviant.

After what seems like an eternity, Jesus slowly rises to his feet, and He speaks the words that echo this very day to the accusers of the monsters.

"If any one of you is without sin, let him be the first to throw a stone at her." (vs. 7)

The men don't flinch. I see them raising their arms again, stones in hand, ready to launch them. But Jesus stoops and writes on the ground again. He writes a bit longer. I see Him writing more quickly, more intently.

So, what did Jesus write on the ground? I'd love to know. Someone has speculated that Jesus wrote out some of the sins of the men holding the stones, ready to kill her. Something like "I know what you did last summer." Or, "I know your thoughts when you peeped in on her to confirm her adultery." It's an attractive theory to me, for all the wrong reasons, because I really want these "monsters" to get their due, to be shamed like they're shaming this woman. Sigh. I'm not immune to "monster" thinking myself. The Bible doesn't tell us what Jesus wrote.

But the Bible does tell us what the men did in response to what Jesus said and what He wrote.

"At this, those who heard began to go away one at a time, the older ones first, until only Jesus was left, with the woman still standing there." (vs. 8)

They were forced to remember their own evil. Their own day of judgment before a righteous God. Their own hypocrisy.

The invariable problem with "monster" language and thinking is the subtle conclusion that other people's sins are more heinous and evil than my own. That they're inferior to me. That I can talk about them as harshly and hatefully as I want. That they deserve God's judgment more than I. That they're monsters and I'm not.

It's a great evil and a grave danger for partly wrong people to think they're better than other partly wrong people. There are monsters, and then there's me. There are people who desperately need God's grace, and then there's me. There are people who ought not be allowed to live, and then there's me.

Jesus isn't suggesting that her adultery isn't serious. He later calls on her to "leave her life of sin." He's not calling us to blow past any sin as if it's simply "twenty minutes of action." He's calling all partly wrong people to see their own partly wrong as serious, to cease ranking sins, and to stop the hate, judgmentalism, arrogance and hypocrisy that invariably flow from such rankings.

Nasty labels for other partly wrong people don't help. In fact, they're much more likely to reinforce a belief that "those people" are less than I am, that I'm free to treat them differently than I want to be treated. If they've abused, I can verbally assault them. If they've been hateful, I can unleash hate on them. After all, they're a monster. A piece of shit. A pile of trash.

So what should we call them? How about "almost as broken as I am"? That feels over the top, doesn't it? Even offensive. But it's a phrase God pressed into my heart years ago, and I use it often. It's an adaptation of the Apostle Paul's "I am the chief of sinners" claim. God gave me a way of making it personal to me. Brock's almost as screwed up as I am. She's almost as broken as I am. I'm still not thrilled with it, but it's a vivid reminder of how desperately broken I am, and it keeps my heart more gracious toward other partly wrong people, helping me to love them as I love my own partly wrong self.

We can be too hard on others, but it's also possible to be too hard on ourselves. Parents are especially prone to self-bashing, and there's often a cost for their kids.

Chapter Thirteen

***

OF COURSE PARENTS ARE SCREWY

Two years ago, my oldest son, Roger, graced my Father's Day with a lengthy email detailing specific events where I'd blessed him. He recalled one of our U-Haul trips:

"I think one of my earliest memories of us together was in the moving truck as we headed north. You probably gave me some words of wisdom on that trip, but unfortunately being in the truck distracted me, so while you said, "Son, think about this...", all I heard was "big truck, big truck, oooo, big truck". But, see, the importance of that story is that you let me ride in the big truck with you. You easily could have had me stay in the car with Mom. I imagine I wasn't the easiest rider at times, but you let me ride anyways. Although, I am peeved that you didn't let me drive. But, given that it is Father's Day, we'll let that one slide for now."

His email was full of other words of encouragement. I read it several times a day! Exaggeration? OK, but I have re-read it. Mostly, I read it to counter the memories I have of mistakes and tears and frustration I created for my children. Parents have a kind of indelible memory of their failures with their children. Failure memories invariably eclipse and block any light from the "did something right" moments. Failure memories dominate.

I have many. There's the time(s) I punished the wrong kid. The time I forced a child to eat spinach to the point of gagging. The time I wrongly accused a child of lying. The time I pulled the car over and reamed out one of my kids for simply being scared, reducing the child to tears. How desperately I'd love a parenting do-over for the angry outbursts, the false accusations, the wrong assumptions, and the misguided rules.

This is why parents desperately need to hear from their kids what they did, or are doing, right. The memories they can't escape are the things they did wrong. The grace of my son's letter was the reminder that I was only partly wrong.

Still, I hate being wrong as a parent. I love my kids, but I know that my failures leave marks. That's hard to live with. Getting it wrong with our children is different than almost any other kind of failure. The self-talk that comes from such failures is especially harsh.

I'm such a loser.
My kids deserve better.
I'm not fit to be a parent.
I'm ruining my kids, and they're probably going to become axe-murderers.

Even worse, parenting failures create a temptation to retreat or disappear, creating even greater pain. The dad, haunted by his angry tirades, buries himself in his work, avoiding his children. The mother, grieved by her anxious controlling, finds peace in a wine bottle. Partly wrong with your kids is a terrible weight that can set the stage for even more damage.

Don't let it.

What may help is the realization that your wrongs can set the stage for some rights. Your wrongs can create losses for your children, but they can also create blessings. Stay with me.

In the Father's Day email I mentioned earlier, my son, Roger, would later thank me for admitting I was wrong. My daughter, Carrye, echoed this same theme in her autobiographical book, Gray Faith: "Two of the greatest gifts my parents gave me were their willingness to think critically about the applications of faith they had grown up with, and their ability to admit over time their own shortcomings and faulty beliefs." (Carrye Burr, Gray Faith, Less to Be More, 2016)

My daughter says that one of the greatest gifts we gave her was our ability to admit our wrong behaviors and our wrong ideas. Our partly wrong enabled us to give her an invaluable gift that she couldn't have gotten otherwise. Our partly wrong enabled us to repent, to apologize, to confess. I love her gracious and accurate words "over time." Strugglers that we are, our admitting wasn't always immediate, but when it came, it was a gift. A good. A source of blessing.

Oddly enough, our wrongs can be a gift to our children. Failures create a teachable moment that we'll miss if we retreat. Your wrongs and mistakes give you a chance to talk to your children about anger and addiction and humility and grace and forgiveness and mercy and confession—conversations that can indelibly mark their lives for good.

Your frailty and weaknesses—when acknowledged—are an invitation for your children to share their own fears and struggles and failures. I've been both stunned and humbled by some of the deep personal struggles my children have shared with me through the years. It's a trust and gift almost too great for words, and I tear up thinking about it now, but I realize that I had to be a screw-up myself (and be honest about it) for those moments to happen. My partly wrongs set the stage for some wonderful partly right moments with my children.

Here's yet another gift of partly wrong parents. Three of my kids are parents now themselves, with their own failures, frustration and negative self-talk. But they can never honestly say, "I'm the only struggling parent." They can always look back at their parents and find a strange comfort. My parents screwed stuff up too. They yelled and overreacted and worried and neglected and overcontrolled too. If Joy and I had been "always right" parents, our kids would sense an impossibly high bar in their own parenting.

So, stop trying to be the perfect parent. It isn't possible or healthy. When you became a parent, you instantly joined the partly wrong parent club. And your membership is never revoked, even after all of your kids have left home... if in fact that actually happens. Don't mope over your failures or dwell on them. And whatever you do, don't retreat from your kids. Instead, confess and entrust your failures to God's grace. Acknowledge them to your children. Let your partly wrongs become an opportunity for grace and good.

***

When I was young, my parents taught me the Ten Commandments. The weirdest one, hands down, was that command about idols, though I wasn't thrilled with the "honor your parents" one either. If there was one command that wasn't really needed today, I was sure it was that idol command. Turns out I was wrong.

Chapter Fourteen

***

WHEN GOD AGREES WITH YOU ON EVERYTHING

Repent.

There's a word we don't use very often. Yet it was one of the first instructions Jesus ever gave.

"From that time on Jesus began to preach, 'Repent, for the kingdom of heaven has come near.'" (Matthew 4:17)

So, what does it mean to repent? It means to change your

thinking and your direction. It means to change your course.

I've traveled often through Atlanta, GA. Interstate travel through Atlanta is almost always a challenge. It's a nightmare when there's a fire, complete with billowing black smoke, burning beneath the interstate. Fortunately, this is not a common occurrence, but it happened on March 30, 2017, late in the afternoon. As a fire grew beneath an I-85 overpass, troopers began to advise drivers to turn around, because they were concerned about the integrity of the overpass.

The troopers were asking drivers on I-85 to repent. The road you're on will lead to trouble; for your own good, you need to turn around and take a different route. It may look fine to you, but it's not safe. Turn around. Repent.

I wonder what I would've done if I'd been driving down that stretch of I-85. I know for sure that I wouldn't have wanted to turn around on I-85. It would be a nightmare to find a way to get around to the other side. I also wouldn't have been overly concerned about the fire. I mean, what's a fire going to do to concrete? If allowed by the trooper, I probably would have driven on ahead. And this book wouldn't have been written. I'd be dead. Minutes after troopers began turning cars around, the northbound overpass collapsed, and the repentant drivers were saved.

The story lends context to this word from Jesus: *"I tell you, no! But unless you repent, you too will all perish."* *(Luke 13:3)*

Jesus calls everyone to repentance. But why do we need to repent? Well, we're in danger. But why exactly are we in danger? Because we're wrong. Because something that seems good to us isn't good. We're mistaken. Our thinking is mistaken. Our choices are mistaken. We're wrong. And partly wrong people must repent or face serious consequences. Jesus is the official flagging us down and warning us to turn around.

Partly wrong people must be prepared to repent every single time God shows them that they're wrong.

Every single time. Now, you may have thought that repenting is something you do once—you know, that singular foundational decision you make to turn from a life of doing things your way and choose instead to trust Jesus and follow His way. You've thought repentance is that one point at which you turn to enter into the kingdom of heaven. Boom. Your repenting days are over.

Make no mistake, that first step you take to follow the way of Jesus is pivotal, and it re-shapes the course of your life. But it begins a journey of allowing the instruction and commands of the Father to re-shape you time and time and time again. It launches you into a life of repentance in which you repeatedly discover thinking or choices that don't fit the way of Jesus. At each point, you repent. You shift what you think is best to what He thinks is best. You shift your behavior to match God's behavior.

This repenting we do regularly. Why? Well, because we're partly wrong. Having turned to follow Jesus, some of our ideas are good and right. Some of our behaviors match the heart of God. Others don't, and as we discover those, we must change to fit God.

That is what we should do, but we are tempted to do something very different...and very dangerous. It's so common and so serious that God specifically warns against it in the Ten Commandments. The problem is that most people read right past the command, thinking it's for someone else. So, here's the word almost no one thinks is for them.

"You shall not make for yourself an idol in the form of

anything in heaven above or on the earth beneath or in the waters below. You shall not bow down to them or worship them; for I, the LORD your God, am a jealous God..." (Exodus 20:4-5)

Before I go any further, I want to talk about God being jealous. Hmmm. Doesn't that sound like a bad thing? When we think of the word jealous, we might think of someone who'is paranoid, over-protective, selfish, and controlling. That's one dimension of jealousy and it's an ugly, destructive thing. But jealousy isn't always negative. The New English Translation has this note: "The word 'jealous' is the same word often translated 'zeal' or 'zealous.' The word describes a passionate intensity to protect or defend something that's jeopardized." God gives commands one and two because He's passionately concerned about our well-being.

In the first and core command, God requires that we love Him above any other deity, person, or thing. God requires that we put him in first place in our lives and decisions-- not because He's power-hungry--but because putting any other person, thing, or deity in first place will jeopardize us. It's for this same reason that He gives us command two: don't make an idol of God and worship it.

And this is the command we always skim by. Why?
Probably no one reading my words has formed a god figure
out of wood or clay and bowed down to it. So we think
something like: "This is for those people in superstitious
countries that form figures to worship. On to command
three."

Hang on. Do you really think that God's core concern is
carving little figures, a trivial little instruction only
directed to some countries you think are a bit primitive?
Let's think more deeply here. What's the big deal?

What happens when you craft a "god" statue or figure?
You make him the way that you want him to be. If you
want him to be a harsh rule-giver, you shape him that way.
If you want a doting grandmother-type, you shape her that
way. You make a god who fits you. You make a god who
pleases you. The core danger of crafting a god is the
deadly idea that the shape of god is something you decide.
I would summarize the second command this way:

We must not shape God into an image of our liking, but we
must allow the reality of God to reshape us.

We must allow the reality of God to reshape us. That's
repentance. When we encounter a difference between God

and us, we must change. But we can do just the opposite. We can simply change God. We make a god that pleases us. It's like going to a restaurant buffet. You get a plate, go down the food line, and do what? You pick out the foods you like. You fix a plate that's comfortable for you. Your plate will look different than mine, because I like different things.

We do the same with God. We look at a table full of all the things that God could be, and we make a god plate we like. "I'll take the god of love, equality, with a side of happiness, hold the anger and judgment please." Someone else will serve up a different god. "I'll take a god of fire and brimstone who demands that people keep the rules." My god's against abortion. My god's for choice. My god's against homosexuality. My god's against divorce. My god's for it.

We're making our own gods, American style. How audacious and insulting and dangerous it is to make God like we want Him to be. When Moses encountered the booming voice of God in a fiery bush, He asked what God called himself and how he should announce God to his people. God's answer: "I am that I am." (Exodus 3:14) He didn't say, "I'm whoever you decide I'll be." God isn't clay that must give way to us. He's a rock to which we must give way. We dare not glibly decide who He'll be.

We must not shape God into an image of our liking, but we must allow the reality of God to reshape us.

So, what should our response be? What does it look like to let God reshape us? We must follow and surrender to God as He is and acts in the pages of the Bible. We must let Him say who He is. We must see and trust His actions. We must heed His warnings, not dismiss them. We must bend to His instructions.

Jesus taught us to pray to the Father: "Your will be done" (Matthew 6:10), even when it's hard or we don't fully understand. It's only as we surrender to the God Who Is that we can be saved. Partly wrong people like us must be repent-ers who allow the reality of God to reshape us, and not the other way around.

I get concerned when I'm talking to someone, and it seems like God agrees with them on everything. Everything they're for, he's for. Everything they're against, he's against. Gun control. Abortion. Immigration. Pornography. Divorce. You name it. By some remarkable coincidence, God has exactly every view that they have. It seems like nothing God says has ever made them uncomfortable. I want to ask: Is it possible you've made god into who you want Him to be?

Almost thirty-six years ago, I asked Joy out for our first date, which turned into another date and then another and then a deep friendship. I loved being with her; I loved being close to her. I read in the pages of the Bible and in the words of Jesus that sexual intimacy was designed for marriage, designed solely for that committed relationship. Honestly, I wanted that not to be true. I didn't understand such an instruction. What's the big deal? It seemed like there was no real harm. I disagreed with God, but I decided to let Him shape me (repentance) rather than me to re-shape Him to fit what I wanted. That was painfully hard, but Joy and I have never regretted that.

We must not shape God into an image of our liking, but we must allow the reality of God to reshape us.

If God agrees with you on everything, it could be that "god" is simply the person you see in the mirror each morning, a god who never thinks differently, never challenges you, never corrects you, and ultimately never saves you from yourself. Remember that the god who's no bigger than you can never save you.

So, consider this question. Does God agree with you on
everything? When you read the words of God and
encounter something you disagree with, do you change
your thinking or behavior(repent) or do you get out your
clay and change your god? The clay should be in His
hands, not ours. It is the partly wrong who need re-
shaping and not God.

We must not shape God into an image of our liking, but we
must allow the reality of God to reshape us.

Allowing God to reshape us is hard, which is why you may
want to just skip the next chapter, where I unpack one of
the hardest teachings of Jesus to accept and obey.

Chapter Fifteen

***

THE ONE TIME YOU'RE ALWAYS RIGHT

The act was brutally evil. Drunk and high, Rusty Woomer and a friend went on a terrible rampage. In a spree of robberies and murder, they raped and killed a convenience store clerk, Della Summers. Her murder landed Rusty on South Carolina's death row, where he languished, zombie-like, in a filthy, roach-infested cell. A persistent visitor shared the preposterous idea that God could forgive someone like Rusty. Clinging to that good news and the pardon of Jesus, Rusty gradually experienced a transformation of heart and life that no one could quite believe, not even his warden and guards.

Still aching from the immeasurable pain and losses he created for others, he wrote tearful apologies to the families of all his victims. As you might expect, no one responded. For years. Then one day, a letter was placed in his hands. He tensed, seeing that it was from Lee Hewitt, brother of Della Summers. He forced himself to rip the envelope and endure the scathing words that would come.

"For years, I hated you with all my heart," it read in part. "I could have blown your brains out for what you did to my sister. I only regretted that you were in prison where I couldn't get to you. But I've spent time in jail myself—56 times over the years. I felt like a failure. But then I became a Christian. And the more I learned about being a Christian,, the more I knew that I had to forgive you....Now the ball was in my court. I've prayed about it, and God has done a miracle in my heart. I forgive you. We are brothers in Christ. I love you." (Chuck Colson, The Body, Word Publishing, 1992, pp. 400-401))

I know that such a story stirs intense emotions and knotty questions. One question sure to be asked is whether it's ever right or even healthy to extend that kind of forgiveness. And so I ask you: Should Lee have forgiven Rusty? When should you forgive and when should you not forgive?

I'm not wise nor brave enough to answer that question on my own, but Jesus is. Better still, someone asked him that very question and, best of all, he braved an answer, which means we don't have to guess what how He *might* have answered the question. We know how He *did* answer the question. Oh, and guess who asked the question? It's our good, partly wrong friend, Peter.

"Then Peter came to Jesus and asked, 'Lord, how many times shall I forgive my brother when he sins against me? Up to seven times?'"(Matthew 18:21)

I love Peter. He poses a question and immediately offers an answer. He just can't help himself. But it's a generous answer. Seven times. And seven is the number of perfection, I'm told. I'm guessing he thought Jesus would praise his answer; after all, that'd happened before. Peter's answer sorta went this way. You don't have to forgive if the person won't stop hurting you. Forgive those first few offenses. Give them a chance to straighten up. But there's a limit. Perhaps the limit should be seven? Turns out that Jesus had a different number in mind.

"Jesus answered, 'I tell you, not seven times, but seventy-seven times.'" (vs. 22)

I would love to have seen Peter's face at this moment. That's twisted of me, I know, but I do wonder how it hit him. Peter framed a math question. Some think Jesus' answer was addition: 77 times. Some believe his answer was multiplication: 490 (70x7) times. But Jesus wants to be clear that this isn't a math question with a math answer. Instead, it's a justice question with a fairness answer. So Jesus immediately turns his answer into a story rather than an equation.

"Therefore, the kingdom of heaven is like a king who wanted to settle accounts with his servants. As he began the settlement, a man who owed him ten thousand talents was brought to him." (vss. 23-24)

One of the pictures of sin or offense in the Bible is debt. We sometimes use debtor type language when we've been wronged or when a crime has been committed. "She's going to have to pay for what she did to me." "He has to pay his debt to society." "She owes me." Of course, some crimes or violations actually have a fine—a literal monetary debt. And people's fines and fees can add up.

That's what happens in Jesus' story.

The man has sinned against the king repeatedly and has incurred substantial fines or fees or tickets. This man's story is our story. We've sinned against God; We've ignored His warnings and disobeyed His instructions. Every time we've wounded someone, we've also wounded God. We, like this man, are debtors. Serious debtors. How serious, Roger?

The man's debt is ten thousand talents. In the language of modern day American currency, we'd call this "a boatload of money." The NIV Bible note simply says, "millions of dollars." In short, this was an unpayable debt. There was NO WAY this guy was going to "scrounge up that kind of money." Our debt to God is similarly unpayable. We simply don't have the means. We're screwed. Jesus' listeners know this guy is doomed.

So let's try something that may help you to better feel the weight of this story. I'd like you to get out a piece of paper and something to write with. Humor me. Now, write down some of the ways in which you've sinned against God. Remember that every sin against another person is also a sin against God. You're actually creating a kind of ledger or listing of your sins or debts to God. You could also call this your "partly wrong" list.

In order to help you, I've created a starter list, something which can perhaps help spur your memory. If you're reading this along with someone else, don't read their list or recommend additions to it. You should have plenty enough work to do on your own list.

Possible sins or debts: adultery, gossip, rage, drunkenness, hate, lying, ignoring God, gluttony, coveting, slander, cursing someone, revenge, greed, mocking someone, pride, stinginess, disobeying parents, arrogance, breaking a promise, murder, stealing, cheating, jealousy, judging others, ingratitude, rape, ignoring the poor, divisive arguments, tempting someone to sin, cursing God, abusing someone, threatening language, heartlessness, unforgiveness, prostitution, swindling someone, failure to give, assault, lust, trouble-making, unkindness, keeping track of people's wrongs, false accusation, drug abuse, ignoring Sabbath, worshiping idols, ridicule, disobeying the law, selfishness, rudeness, loving money, shoplifting, impatience, angry words, enjoying someone's hurt, failure to admit wrong, bitterness, unwholesome language, rebellious spirit, neglecting your children, ignoring your supervisor, failure to praise God, improper joking, failure to love your spouse, boasting, planning sin, not loving God with all your heart, not loving others like you love yourself, withholding mercy, etc.

For deeper impact, you might even look at certain items on your list and try to guess how "often" you've done those things in your lifetime. Having finished your list (and it's at least possible you've missed a "few" things), you've at least some sense of your indebtedness to God, things you must pay for. O.K., let's get back to Jesus' story.

"Since he was not able to pay, the master ordered that he and his wife and his children and all he had be sold to repay the debt. The servant fell on his knees before him, 'Be patient with me,' he begged, 'and I will pay back everything.'"(vss. 25-26)

After checking the man's accounts and seeing that he couldn't possibly pay, the King orders that everything he owns be sold to recoup some fraction of his massive debt. The man will lose everything he possesses. Desperate, he begs for mercy, with the foolish promise that he'll eventually pay back the debt. Ah yes. Desperate people say desperate, unreasonable things. The tension in this story rises. Now, what will this king do?

"The servant's master took pity on him, canceled the debt

and let him go." (vs. 27)

Several years ago, I was enjoying a party where my birthday was being celebrated. A long-time friend pulled me to the side and said, "My wife and I have decided to cancel the loan we gave you some time back. We want you to have that money." It was a four-figure debt! I know what it's like to have a sizable debt canceled. I was stunned and deeply touched. But what if my friend had said, "We want to do even more. We're going to pay off all your debt —your mortgage, your loans, your credit cards. We want you to be entirely debt-free." I would've been speechless— not a small feat!

This King cancels a debt that this man had no chance of repaying. Can you imagine what he must have felt? Maybe I can help. Take a long look at the ledger sheet you drew up a few minutes ago. Now write "paid in full" in large capital letters across the page. That's what God offers to do for us if we'll seek Him for mercy. He forgives a debt we've no chance in hell of repaying. The King's generosity is staggering, perhaps even ridiculous. The man's able to walk out of the palace entirely debt free, wholly forgiven. But the story isn't finished.

"But when that servant went out, he found one of his

fellow servants who owed him a hundred silver coins."
(vs. 28)

Having just left the palace, the man bumps into a man at
the food market and recognizes him immediately. The guy
owes him 100 denarii. From what I've read, this may be
ten dollars. Again to help you feel the weight of the story,
I'd like you to get a paper and pen again. I know that you
have "writer's cramp" from the first list, but please humor
me and create a second ledger.

I want you to think of one specific person who has
wronged you. A name may immediately come to mind, but
don't write the name down. I would, however, like for you
to write down how that person has hurt you. This could be
called your "partly wronged" list. Now, this may be
someone you've already forgiven, or it may be someone
you struggle to forgive almost every day of your life, or it
may be someone you feel you can't forgive right now.
Below, I've created a starter list of some possible hurts and
losses someone may have inflicted on you.

Someone...lied to you, lied about you, broke a promise,
abused you, "ruined" your life, failed to admit wrong,
harsh words, conned you of money, abandoned you, killed
someone you love, mocked you, injured you, stole your

spouse/good friend, took advantage of you, cheated on you, raped you, falsely accused you, attacked you, publicly humiliated you, assaulted you, divorced you, divorced someone you love, etc.

O.K., let's go back to the food market outside the palace.

"He grabbed him and began to choke him. 'Pay back what you owe me!' he demanded. His fellow servant fell to his knees and begged him, 'Be patient with me, and I will pay you back.' But he refused. Instead, he went off and had the man thrown into prison until he could pay the debt. When the other servants saw what had happened, they were greatly distressed and went and told their master everything that had happened." (vss. 28-31)

Borrowing the title of a classic *Reader's Digest* feature: That's Outrageous! It angers me every time I read it. Well, that was the response of the king as well.

"Then the master called the servant in. 'You wicked servant,' he said, 'I canceled all that debt of yours because you begged me to. Shouldn't you have had mercy on your fellow servant just as I had on you?'" (vss. 32-33)

So take a look at the two ledgers you've written out: your

"partly wrong" list and your "partly wronged" list. If God has fully forgiven your lengthy "partly wrong" list, it's unreasonable, even outrageous, for you not to forgive that person who has wronged you. It's true that some of you have been viciously wounded, cheated, or violated—far beyond my ability to comprehend. I'm not lightly dismissing that, but the point of Jesus' story is that the ledger of offense against you will never be greater than your ledger sheet of offense against God. Never. If your list of "that person's" offenses against you is longer than your list against God, you've forgotten some things...a lot of things.

Forgiving any less than God forgives us is scandalous, really. This is what Lee Hewitt came to realize. No one in the world would blame him for withholding forgiveness, and some would find his mercy to be...well, unforgivable. But he came to see that he was that deeply forgiven man who was refusing to forgive his fellow man.

You might protest that Rusty's actions were gross evil, and you're right. But it's part of our own broken condition that we fail to see how gross our own evil is. When I resolve not to forgive, I've grossly underestimated my own sin and need for forgiveness. God's not minimizing the wrong done to me, but when I choose not to forgive, I'm minimizing my evils which God has forgiven.

So, Jesus, whom should I forgive? Every person who wrongs you. Every time.

The partly wrong person fully forgiven by God must extend that same full forgiveness to those who wrong them. It may take days or even years of repeated forgiveness. It may require a choice to forgive every day of your life, but God's persistent forgiveness compels it. It's only reasonable. It's only right. It's always right.

***

I'm a big fan of Adam Scott's Dilbert cartoon series. Maybe too big, because I managed to work one of his cartoons into the next chapter.

Chapter Sixteen

***

I HUMBLY ADMIT THAT YOU'RE WRONG

Scott Adam's Dilbert cartoons are brilliantly funny because they're so true to life. In a February, 2013 cartoon, he offered this classic exchange between an employee and the Pointy-Haired Boss:

Employee: _"The CEO of Apple says we should admit when we are wrong. That won't work for me because I'm never wrong. The best I can do is admit when other people are wrong."_

Pointy haired boss: *"That sort of misses the point."*
Employee: *"Well, I humbly admit you're wrong."*
(Scott Adams, Dilbert.com, Feb 20, 2013)

The employee is us. None of us actually say we're never wrong, but all of us act like it from time to time. And since we aren't wrong, it has to be somebody else that's wrong. So we deny or blame or accuse or correct. We're forced to "humbly" submit that someone else is wrong.

Just the other day, I reached for the salt shaker to enhance a dish I was cooking on the stovetop. The salt shaker wasn't in its spot, which was first frustrating my cooking, and then me. I thought, "Why does Joy do that?" After all, it's not that complicated to put the salt right back in its spot. By chance, and God's humor, I glanced out our back door window to see the salt shaker on the back deck table... right where I'd left it during an earlier scorched green bean fiasco.

I'd instinctively assumed Joy was wrong. Obviously, I couldn't have been. I was that cartoon employee, happily admitting that somebody else was wrong. I wish this only happened with trivial things like salt shakers, car keys and remotes. But I default to this self-assured thinking with ideas that matter a great deal. The person in the wrong is anyone but me.

Religious people are especially prone to such overconfidence, humbly or not-so-humbly admitting that everyone else is wrong. Forgive me in advance for using a story about the Pharisees in the Bible. They're an easy mark for those of us who think we're nothing like them, but I use their story because we're much more like them than we realize.

The Pharisees were a group of Israel's religious leaders and teachers in Jesus' day. They had a passion to see that Israel followed God's laws to the letter, and in the process, they added a few of their own letters to that law, especially with how the Sabbath, Israel's weekly holy day, should be honored. They created quite a few Sabbath laws, one of which forbade anyone to heal someone on that holy day.

There was a day, then, when Jesus healed a blind man. Jesus gave the gift of sight to a man whose entire life had been reduced to begging on the streets. Suddenly, people had that same beggar run up to them, look them in the eye, and tell them what was already clear: he could see. Jesus was apparently not paying attention to the calendar; He healed the man on the Sabbath. The remarkable healing story spread rapidly, finding its way to the Pharisees, who had to investigate, especially since it was a forbidden Sabbath healing. They first heard the detailed story from the smiling, blinking man himself. And the Bible has this to say about their first thoughts:

"Some of the Pharisees said, 'This man is not from God, for he does not keep the Sabbath.' But others asked, 'How can a sinner perform such signs?' So they were divided." (John 9:16)

Some drew an immediate conclusion. This Jesus doesn't keep our Sabbath laws. He doesn't agree with us. So he can't possibly be from God. But there was this small problem. He had just healed a man born blind, an eye-opening miracle.

Here was their opportunity to think: Maybe our ideas about the Sabbath are partly wrong.

You can see their wrestling. This sure looks like something someone from God does. On the other hand, He's disregarding God's Sabbath laws (Pharisaic edition). Hmmm. Either he's wrong or we're wrong. And here's the sad, haunting reality. Though there was strong evidence they could be wrong, they couldn't envision that possibility. So, they humbly admitted everyone else was wrong.

When you don't think you can be wrong, and evidence suggests you are, you will begin grasping for explanations. Here was their first: This guy is lying about having been blind. So, they went to his parents. They weren't subtle. *"Is this your son? Is this the one you say was born blind?"* (vs. 19) Listen to the implication. We humbly admit that you're wrong. The parents insist he was their boy who'd never seen a human face before that Sabbath.

Grasping at a new theory, they went back to visit the ex-beggar. Maybe he actually had been blind, but now he's *lying* about Jesus healing him. That was it. So they announced: *"Give glory to God by telling the truth,...we know this man is a sinner."* (vs. 24) We know. We're certain. We can't be wrong. Which can only mean one thing. We humbly admit that you're wrong. They couldn't see that they might be wrong. That wasn't an option.

The Pharisees, in this moment, ought to be a sobering lesson to us all, but here's the comic, ironic reality. Almost no one thinks they could be a Pharisee. We can't possibly make the same mistake. Christians can be the worst in this regard. After all, we know the Bible. But that's EXACTLY what those Pharisees thought. Because they knew the Law, they couldn't possibly be wrong. Similarly, Christians, Bibles in hand, are prone to assume they're always right. This may be an even greater danger when you've a title like teacher or professor or pastor or clergy or adviser or counselor or scholar or apostle.

I think of Peter. I'm guessing he wouldn't consider himself a Pharisee. But when Jesus told the disciples that the Messiah must die, Peter said the same thing the Pharisees did: I humbly admit that you're wrong. The Bible's actual wording indicates he rebuked Jesus. *"This shall never happen to you, Lord."* (Matthew 16:22)

Here was Peter's opportunity to think: "Maybe my ideas about the Messiah are partly wrong."

He had the chance to say to Jesus: I'm confused. Help me understand why God would allow the Messiah to be killed, because it seems wrong to me. Help me see where I'm partly wrong. But he blew by that possibility with a rebuke: I humbly admit that you—the Messiah!—are wrong.

Don't laugh at Peter; we do it all the time. Or are you that person who doesn't struggle with a single teaching of Jesus? I recall talking to someone about Jesus' call for us to forgive, and she said "well, he wasn't talking about situations like mine." Another way to say: I humbly admit that you're wrong. To Jesus. We read what Jesus says about marriage or hell or divorce or loving our enemies (like ISIS) or taking in immigrants or visiting prisoners or caring for the poor or loving him more than our own family, and it doesn't sound or feel right.

It creates an opportunity for us to think: Maybe my ideas about hell or divorce or forgiveness or sex are wrong.

In such moments, we're really faced with the same conundrum the Pharisees felt. That Peter experienced. Either God's wrong or I'm wrong. If we're sure that we can't possibly be wrong, we won't pause. We'll either correct Jesus or reject Him. We'll either throw Him out entirely: "I can't possibly follow the way of Jesus if he would send someone to hell." Or we'll correct Him: "I don't think he actually said that" or "surely He didn't mean that" or "He understands my situation is different." I humbly admit that you're wrong.

If you and I disagree with God, we're certainly wrong. If we disagree with others, we may be wrong. This can be even harder to accept. And if we sometimes think we know better than God, we absolutely will think we know better than mere mortals.

We must fight the pervasive assumption that we're right, even though we've been wrong countless times. So, how do we do that? Change the pronoun. I humbly admit that *I* may be wrong. Maybe we should actually use those very words from time to time.

A few years back, my brother Bruce tried opening up conversations with the words, "I'm probably wrong, but..." That's not a bad option either. If nothing else, it's great for the shock value. We need words that keep us in a humble posture.

I never like to correct people or address conflicts in relationships, but love and the instructions of Jesus require that we have those conversations. Embracing my partly wrong, I start them differently now: "I have a concern, but before I share it, I want to say that I may have misread something. It's possible I am overreacting. I may have made an assumption that's wrong. I care, but I may be wrong."

What if we opened conversations about religion or politics or gun control or immigration or abortion or prison reform or race relations with "I humbly admit I may be wrong about some of this" kind of language? Well, for starters, we could actually have a meaningful conversation. And in that conversation, we could discover a flawed idea. And the new idea might save us or someone else.

Sure that everyone else was wrong, some Pharisees missed out on the grace of God that was close enough to touch. And it could've been prevented with one simple admission.

I humbly admit that I may be wrong.

***

Would it be encouraging to hear that some really bright people have been terribly wrong? I thought so. I'm here to help. Maybe you've heard of a guy named Albert Einstein.

PARTLY WRONG

Chapter Seventeen

***

STUPID MAKES YOU HUMBLE

On a recent morning beach walk in New Smyrna Beach, Florida, I came across the fresh marks of a sea turtle which had, overnight, come up the beach to create a nesting area for her eggs. It was the most odd, meandering route I'd ever seen a turtle leave, as if the turtle had been drinking, though I know a pregnant turtle would *not* be drinking. The turtle preservation staff drove up minutes later, checking a spot where the eggs might be. Thinking they might looking in the wrong spot, I theorized out loud how the turtle came up the beach, carefully describing her movements as seen in the sand. One team member, graciously avoiding the word "obvious," pointed out that the direction of the flipper marks made my claim impossible. Ouch. Not only was I comically wrong, I was correcting trained staff who do this all the time! I quietly slipped away, mumbling at my foolishness.

I wasn't wrong to make an assessment, to theorize, to draw a conclusion or make a claim. That's a natural part of being human, made in the image of God. Unlike God, however, my claims and conclusions are sometimes wrong. Perhaps to make me feel better about my debunked turtle theory, I'll share a few deductions others have made:

"There is not the slightest indication that nuclear energy will ever be obtainable. It would mean that the atom would have to be shattered at will." – Albert Einstein, 1932

"We don't like their sound, and guitar music is on the way out." – Decca Recording Company explaining why they did not sign the Beatles, 1962

"This 'telephone' has too many shortcomings to be seriously considered as a means of communication. The device is inherently of no value to us." – Western Union internal memo, 1876

"I think there is a world market for maybe five computers."
– Thomas Watson, chairman of IBM, 1943

"Everyone acquainted with the subject will recognize it as
a conspicuous failure." – -Henry Morton, president of the
Stevens Institute of Technology, regarding Thomas
Edison's light bulb, 1880

"The horse is here to stay but the automobile is only a
novelty—a fad." – -The president of the Michigan Savings
Bank to the lawyer of Henry Ford, 1903

"Television won't last because people will soon get tired of
staring at a plywood box every night." – -Darryl Zanuck,
movie producer, 20th Century Fox, 1946

"The wireless music box has no imaginable commercial
value. Who would pay for a message sent to no one in
particular?" – -Associates of David Sarnoff, who in 1921
was urged to invest in radio

(Source for the quotes above: list25.com/25-famous-
predictions-that-were-proven-to-be-horribly-wrong)

"Summary: Is not what you're looking for in terms of physical stature, strength, arm strength and mobility, but he has the intangibles and production and showed great Griese-like improvement as a senior. Could make it in the right system but will not be for everyone." (NFL Quarterback Tom Brady's pre-draft scouting report, 2000)

The light bulb turned out to be a stunning success, as did automobiles, computers, radio, the Beatles, the telephone, television, and Tom Brady. In fact, people are still listening to the Beatles and Tom Brady on their phones, computers, and radios...in their cars! Someone was wrong. Voiced the wrong idea. Even someone as brilliant as Albert Einstein was badly mistaken. Gosh, that's encouraging. It's easy to laugh about the ridiculously wrong ideas of others, but we probably shouldn't. Because all of us have made claims that looked silly later. Remember the sea turtle.

Being wrong is humbling. This is one great gift of being wrong. Humility. Or at it can be, if we'll pay attention. Every wrong idea and conclusion and claim is a reminder of the limits of my understanding, discernment, and knowledge. None of us escape being ignorant or mistaken. We only know so much. Honestly, in the big picture of things, we know very little. Every day exposes things we don't know. Every week surfaces mistaken ideas. Our history of wrong ideas should keep us humble.

In a memorable commencement address, author David Foster Wallace reminded newly degreed graduates: "The point here is that I think this is one part of what teaching me how to think is really supposed to mean. To be just a little less arrogant. To have just a little critical awareness about myself and my certainties. Because a huge percentage of the stuff that I tend to be automatically certain of is, it turns out, totally wrong and deluded. I have learned this the hard way, as I predict you graduates will, too." (David Foster Wallace, *This is Water*, Kenyon College commencement address, 2005)

Unfortunately, staying humble is complicated by our right ideas. My mother was an English teacher. In college, I minored in English. I know a lot about "right" grammar, what words to use and what not to use. I know that "Him and I got drunk" is both bad grammar and a bad idea. I know that irregardless is not a word.

Regardless, people use "irregardless" all the time. It's hard for me not to think "how can you not know that is wrong?" There's this pull to think slightly less of someone who's wrong, which is a nice way of saying that I usually feel superior when I'm right. When I give the right answer in class. When my spouse and I disagree, and I discover I was right. When the boss affirms the statement that I made.

The Bible reminds us that:

"...knowledge puffs up while love builds up." (1 Corinthians 8:1)

Knowledge puffs up. There's a healthy joy and satisfaction in being right, but I can rarely keep it healthy. It tends to inflate my sense of importance and value and superiority to others. "See, I was right," I gloat. I parade my "right ideas" and dismiss my wrong ideas. My right idea is a marker of my superiority. Because my idea is right, I am wiser, more discerning, smarter, better, more attuned to the heart of God than others.

Knowledge puffs up. It's hard not to slight people for what they don't know. We find ourselves saying things like *"Everyone* knows that," a subtle slap in the face to the person who didn't know that. In our worst moments, we may find ourselves snickering at or calling attention to someone's ignorance. "I can't believe anyone wouldn't know that." People understand the translation: "You're

stupid. I'm smart." Knowledge puffs up. It shouldn't, of
course, because of the reminder that follows:

*"...knowledge puffs up while love builds up. Those who
think they know something do not yet know as they ought
to know." (1 Corinthians 8:1-2)*

Pride is foolish because we're all ignorant. We're all partly
wrong. And what we don't know is far greater than what
we do know. How arrogant and foolish and broken it is to
selectively use one thing I got right as a mark of
superiority.

I don't use the word irregardless. Good for me. But I
make other grammatical errors. You won't have to look
hard in this book to find some of them. For all I get right,
there's plenty more I get wrong.

We—the partly wrong—should be humble when we're
right, because there are plenty of things we get wrong.
And there's one final reason why the partly wrong should
be humble.

Anything we ever get right is a gracious gift from God. I
think back to Peter's brilliant declaration to Jesus: *"You
are the Messiah, the Son of the living God."* (Matthew

16:16) Jesus said to him, "Blessed are you." He did not say "Superior are you." No. *"Blessed are you...for this was not revealed to you by flesh and blood, but by my Father in heaven." (Matthew 16:17)*

Peter, you got the answer right, but it wasn't because of your great insight; it was a gift from God. Peter had no place for pride. He was right only because God graced him to be right. The only reason any partly wrong person is ever right is grace. The Apostle Paul affirms this same thing:

For who makes you different from anyone else? What do you have that you did not receive? And if you did receive it, why do you boast as though you did not? (1 Corinthians 4:7)

The insights and right answers and growth you have come from God; they're not because of your brilliance or dedication or spiritual depth. They're ultimately a grace from God.

Partly wrong people should be humble because of their mistakes, errors, and ignorance. Partly wrong people should be humble when they're right, accurate or insightful. Partly wrong people should be humble. It's stupid not to be.

***

I'm told that many people in other countries love to talk about religion. Not so much in America. Starting up a conversation here about Jesus is like raking fingernails across a chalkboard. Part of the discomfort is the ever-controversial Jesus, but another source of the irritation is Christians, and God would like that part to change.

Chapter Eighteen

***

LET'S TALK ABOUT JESUS

Every person on the planet needs Jesus. I believe that. Everyone needs the life and grace and peace and joy and hope and instruction of Jesus, and we who've found that in Him should tell others about him. I mean, how do we not talk about the best thing that ever happened to us? How do we not share good news? And so the Bible says:

Since, then, we know what it is to fear the Lord, we try to persuade others. (2 Corinthians 5:11)

I like the tone of the word "persuade." Some understandably react to a word like "preach" or "convert," which may imply arm-twisting or haranguing. But every person who has ever lived tries to persuade. Children do. "Mommy, if you let me buy it, I'll be good all day. I promise. Pleeeaaase!" Adults do. "Please give me your keys; you're in no condition to drive." Persuading is a part of life. For Christians who've found hope in Jesus, it makes sense that we persuade others to embrace that same hope.

In churchworld, we call it evangelism, a term that stirs mixed emotions in me. It has the beautiful inherent meaning of sharing good news, but the shine has become tarnished. Bible teacher, Steve Brown, says: "We are just beggars telling other beggars where we found bread." That's sounds like good news, but it can subtly morph into bad news: "We're right people telling wrong people how right we are." And that doesn't sound like good news. Reading through the pages of the Bible, I find it more appropriate to say:

We're partly wrong people telling partly wrong people how Jesus can get us right.

The attitude of our heart is so critical, and so the Bible

challenges us: *"But in your hearts revere Christ as Lord. Always be prepared to give an answer to everyone who asks you to give the reason for the hope that you have. But do this with gentleness and respect." (1 Peter 3:15)*

Give an answer...for the hope...with gentleness and respect.

We're to talk about Jesus with gentleness and respect. Here's where awareness of our partly wrong can help us. In the conversation about our hope, we're one partly wrong person talking to another partly wrong person. Or if you prefer. We're one partly right person talking to another partly right person. When it comes to talking about our hope, there's the tendency to believe I'm all right and the other person is all wrong. I remember hearing an evangelism instructor stress that very point.

There are some parts of the good news of Jesus that you don't fully understand nor live out. And the person you are talking to, made in the image of God, is right about some things where you're wrong. A number of years ago, it dawned on me that some of my non-Christian friends reflected more of God's heart for the poor than I did. I had things to learn from them. When I sit down to talk about my hope in Jesus, I must remember: I have some things wrong and my friend has some things right.

C.S. Lewis wrote: "If you're a Christian you do not have to believe that all the other religions are simply wrong all through. If you are an atheist you do have to believe that the main point in all the religions of the whole world is simply one huge mistake. If you're a Christian, you're free to think that all these religions, even the queerest ones, contain at least some hint of the truth." (C.S. Lewis, Mere Christianity, Harper Collins, 1952)

Jesus, in conversations with people, seemed intent on finding what people had right and affirming that before addressing what they might have wrong. A lawyer asked Jesus how to have the hope of eternal life. Jesus immediately asked him what he thought. When the lawyer said that we should love God with all of our hearts and love our neighbor as ourselves, Jesus affirmed his answer. He then addressed the lawyer's wrong idea about which neighbors to love.

A wealthy executive asked Jesus the same question about how to gain eternal life. He expressed a high regard for the Ten Commandments, something Jesus affirmed before exposing a love for money that was greater than his love for God. Jesus entered into a conversation with a gal from

Samaria. She had right ideas; she believed in a coming Messiah. She had wrong ideas about God and worship, which Jesus later corrected.

Jesus was the only "fully right" human to ever walk the planet, and still he didn't talk to people as if they were entirely wrong. He had conversations, not lectures. He listened and asked questions. He blessed what they got right and challenged what they got wrong. Even in intense conversations with some Pharisees, he affirmed things they got right while strongly rebuking their error. Dare we talk to people differently, partly wrong as we are?

An "I'm all right and you're all wrong" posture is not only mistaken, but it's arrogant and repulsive. It feels like a trip to the principal's office. Give an answer for your hope with gentleness and respect, God reminds. With gentleness, as someone who doesn't have it all figured out. With respect, as someone who has something to learn from the other. Do you really believe you have something to learn from every person you encounter? Does that come through in how you talk to people? I love these words from Dallas Willard:

"If I, as a Christian, am going to debate someone who is a non-Christian, I want to be able to put my arm around that person's shoulder and say, 'we are looking for the truth together, and if you can show me where I am wrong, I'll take your side. I'm not there to beat someone into submission. Jesus never worked that way.'" (Dallas Willard, The Allure of Gentleness, Harper Collins, Kindle Edition, pg. 50)

An arm around the shoulder. I love that image. A couple of partly wrong people talking together about how Jesus can make us right. A conversation, not a lecture. Listening, not simply talking. Here are a few thoughts as to how we can talk about Jesus as partly wrong, fellow-learners.

Evangelism, in most of my churchworld experience, was mostly about talking. Most questions we asked simply set the table for our next point. Questions were less about getting to know a person and his/her story than they were about identifying wrong ideas to correct. I am over-generalizing, I'm sure, and I know that the sharers cared about the people they talked to, but I'm not sure the approach always conveyed that love. If we love the people we're telling about Jesus, it makes sense to love them by learning their names and hearing their stories and listening to their ideas. And listening begets listening.

Like Jesus, let's build off of what others get right. Are you talking to a Muslim? Like the Samaritans in Jesus' day, they have right ideas. Some Christians actually use parts of the Koran as they explain the story of Jesus. In discussion with people, you'll surface right things they believe about the power of love, the need for justice, the existence of God, the brokenness of our world, the struggle to do right, or a belief in eternity. As you learn what people believe, you may also be able to show them that some things they believe or practice are in fact more consistent with the Christian narrative than their own. You may also learn places where you are wrong.

Talk honestly about where you and other Christians have gotten things wrong. Share wrong ideas you once believed. Talk about your own arrogance or stinginess or judgmentalism. Acknowledge where the Christian church hasn't reflected the heart and example of Jesus in our racism or harshness or materialism or hatefulness. This is both honest and endearing—identifying ourselves as partly wrong people who are still in need of learning and being changed.

And now we can talk about where we believe our friend may be wrong. Wrong ideas matter, especially when it comes to the way of Jesus. Where my friend disagrees with

Jesus, he/she is mistaken. Love demands that I challenge wrong ideas, just as Jesus did. We, who are partly wrong and have had to repent countless times, must call others to do the same.

Here's where a conversation grounded in compassion, gentleness and respect is so critical. Jesus, in talking to the dear Samaritan woman, said, *"You Samaritans worship what you do not know." (John 4:22)* It was a bold, corrective word, but Jesus had been a caring listener who obviously valued her and her ideas, and ultimately she received that correction and embraced Jesus as the way home to the Father. It's far easier for someone to hear a corrective word when they know they're heard, respected and loved.

We have one unexpected advantage that Jesus didn't have. We're flawed. We've had to repent ourselves. Remembering and admitting our own flawed ideas can become a compelling catalyst for someone else to do the same. Partly wrong people have a wonderful platform to help other partly wrong people come home to the Father.

***

A new question emerges, then. What truths about God

must anyone get right? A doctor or airline pilot can afford to get some things wrong, but there are other things that must be right. We all have some wrong ideas about God, but what response to God must someone get right?

Chapter Nineteen

***

HOW RIGHT MUST YOU BE?

You and I were born into a grand love story. An eternal God—Who has always loved as Father, Son and Spirit—created a magnificent universe and then made humans to love Him and each other forever. Made in His image, we'll never not exist. In order for us to love, the Father gave us choice, for love isn't possible without it. Nor is evil, tragically. And with this precious gift of choice, we've turned from God, disregarded and disobeyed Him, choices both unloving and evil, a violation of both love and justice.

Love demands a punishment for evil, a barricading of the offender from the beautiful, just kingdom and its King, the Father.

The Father determined that the love story wasn't finished. He planned for His eternal Son, Jesus, to be born as a human, walk in our suffering, announce the kingdom, and to die, taking the judgment of the Father for the sins of the created. Jesus joyfully embraced the plan, despite the horrific cost. The Father raised him back to life, ultimately breaking the power of selfishness, hate and death. He offers a pardon to all who'll receive it—to those who return to the Father, believing His love, and trusting the work of the Son. Those who embrace the pardon enjoy life with the Father without end, and the love story continues forever.

That's an impossibly simple summary of the gospel or "good news" of the eternal life of love for which God made us. But how much of that story must one understand, believe, or even know in order to return home to the Father's house, to enjoy the eternal love life for which they were made? Are there pieces of the story beyond my summary that they must know before they can enter?

What must you be right about?

No one is fully right about everything. No one fully understands God and the gospel. Every single person believes wrong things about God and the gospel. To deny that would be the ultimate arrogance. So, what is it that we must be right about? It's perhaps the most precarious question I raise in this book, making this my most challenging chapter, the one in fact that I almost didn't write, but God didn't release me to do otherwise.

I speak as humbly and carefully as I can, knowing full well that I'm partly wrong, leaving it to God Himself to guide each reader to the truth. I'll dare to share a few ideas drawn from the pages of the Bible, confident that God will correct my errors as necessary.

I'll start with this observation. Our distance from God is an issue of our heart more than our mind. It's less about what we know and more about what we love. It's less about believing the wrong things as it is about loving and trusting the wrong things and persons. We haven't loved God with all of our heart, if we've loved Him at all. We haven't loved our neighbors as ourselves. Repentance is a change of heart—a change in what we both trust and love.

I'm saying first that entrance into the kingdom of heaven doesn't hinge on acing a religion test. There's not some designated number of facts one must be right about, as there might be for an attorney to enter the bar, for instance. This isn't to say that facts are unimportant. Knowledge has a vital connection to what we love and trust. Flawed ideas matter, but entering the kingdom of heaven isn't simply a matter of believing right facts. We enter through a change of heart.

Perhaps we can say it this way: We must know enough to move our hearts to love and trust God.

What're the facts or realities that move us to love and trust God? Fundamentally, it starts with God, and so the Bible says,

"And without faith it is impossible to please God, because anyone who comes to him must believe that he exists and that he rewards those who earnestly seek him." (Hebrews 11:6)

'

God exists. He's personal. He wants us to seek Him, and He's responsive. Again, these aren't facts to memorize for an entrance exam. Without this core understanding of God and His heart, you've no idea how to approach him, that you need to, or that He longs for you to. He's a Father who made you to love him and seek Him and speak to Him. He made you, and you're accountable to Him.

What other good news must you know in order to seek Him, repent and move toward Him? The Apostle Paul gives a summary briefer than my earlier attempt.

"By this gospel you are saved, if you hold firmly to the word I preached to you. Otherwise, you have believed in vain. For what I received I passed on to you as of first importance: that Christ died for our sins according to the Scriptures, that he was buried, that he was raised on the third day according to the Scriptures, and that he appeared to Cephas, and then to the Twelve." (1 Corinthians 15:2-5)

Sins. Now there's a controversial word, but it's part of the story. On two different occasions, Jesus is asked what one must do to enter the kingdom of heaven. Jesus never corrects the question to read: What must I know? It is rightly a "what must I do" question. In both cases, the Ten Commandments come up, and Jesus reveals to each how he fails to love God and his neighbor. Jesus gets at what they love and what they trust. God or money. God or themselves. So, what's their sin and ours? We haven't loved God with all of our heart nor have we loved our neighbors as ourselves. The Ten Commandments expose us as sinners, as runaways from the Father's house.

But Jesus died for sinners.

The Jesus part of the story is essential. No one has ever gained entrance into the kingdom of heaven apart from the work of Jesus. Not Abraham. Not Moses. Not Rahab. Not Joshua. Not Ruth. Not David. Not Peter. Not Mary. Not Mother Teresa. Not me. Many have entered the kingdom of heaven without knowing the name of Jesus, but no one has entered without the work of Jesus. No one ever enters the kingdom of heaven apart from His payment for our sins and the Father raising Him from the dead.

We announce Jesus as the astounding love of God to embrace and trust. Jesus, the Son, dying for sinners is the climax of the great love story. Jesus lives out the greatest love ever, and it's love that spurs love in return. And so the Bible says that *"God's kindness is intended to lead you to repentance" (Romans 2:4)* We don't need to hear the story of Jesus for information; We need to hear it for transformation. It's what stirs our hearts to trust and love God, and so the Bible says, *"we love because he first loved us."* (1 John 4:19) The amazing love of Jesus stirs a response. It's why we share the Jesus story.

"For God so loved the world that he gave his one and only Son, that whoever believes in him shall not perish but have eternal life." (John 3:16)

The response is trust. Believe him. Trust Him. Turn to Him. Come back home to the Father. What we must get right is a turn of heart to trust, love and obey God.

My brief summary isn't all there is to the good news story, not even close. There's much more we must learn in order to *"grow in the grace and knowledge of our Lord and Savior Jesus Christ."* (2 Peter 3:18) There's *always* more to learn about Jesus and salvation, but I hesitate to say there are more things someone must know and understand to take that first baby step into the kingdom of God.

What must one get right? In wrestling with the question, it may help to ask the question another way: What must a child understand in order to turn to God? Must a child know or understand that Jesus was born of a virgin? The trinity? (As if any of us fully understands the trinity anyway.) The Holy Spirit? The bodily resurrection of Jesus?

What names of God must one know? Jehovah. I Am?

Immanuel? Christ? Must someone understand the concept of Messiah? Or the Jewish sacrificial system? Must someone initially understand that there's no other way to God outside of Jesus? Might someone mistakenly believe that there's some kind of good work they must do? Must someone understand that Jesus was fully God and fully man at the same time?

I know that the posing of the questions may, for some, sound almost heretical, but I'm not suggesting that these realities are unimportant to the grand salvation story. I'm not saying they needn't be taught over time. I'm not saying that we shouldn't correct wrong ideas; that's part of what it means to grow up in our salvation. I'm not saying that what one believes is inconsequential.

I *am* saying that the gospel is simple enough to be received by a child. I *am* saying that it's possible to trust God and enter His kingdom even when some of what we believe about God and the gospel is mistaken. I *am* saying that God knows and responds to the posture of our hearts even when our knowledge is flawed. I *am* saying that there's not a knowledge-based entrance exam for the kingdom of heaven. I *am* saying that what someone must have right is a change of heart toward God. I *am* saying that the only people who've ever entered the kingdom of heaven are

partly wrong people who then need to be walking in
community with other believers, learning each day other
things they've been getting wrong. I *am* saying that you
needn't have every single thing right in order to come
home to the Father's house. Or no one ever could.

***

Why is it that I struggle to figure out my own motives, but
I can confidently determine anyone else's in a shutter
flash? As much as I get wrong, you'd think I'd hesitate to
assume and attack the motive of another person's heart.
You'd think, but you'd be wrong.

PARTLY WRONG

Chapter Twenty

***

THE MOTIVE POLICE

Perhaps you've heard of the Nashville Statement. It's not a tourist brochure. On August 29, 2017 the document was released by a group of 150+ Christian signatories as a "statement of the core Christian position regarding human sexuality and gender," expressed as 14 affirmations and denials. As you'd expect, there was an immediate social media response. Christian critics tweeted their displeasure and anger.

"The fruit of the 'Nashville Statement' is suffering, rejection, shame, and despair. The timing is callous beyond words." (Jen Hatmaker, Twitter.com, August 29, 2017)

I have my own statement on the #NashvilleStatement. It could be lots of words but honestly I could probably narrow it down to just a finger. (John Pavlovitz, Twitter.com, August 29, 2017)

After #Charlottesville & #Harvey, a bunch of mostly-white, mostly-male evangelicals release a "manifesto" on sexuality. (Shane Claiborne, Twitter.com, August 30, 2017)

Then the Christian supporters of the statement volleyed back.

"I understand that (Rachel Held) Evans is fond of distancing herself from orthodox Christianity – it opens far more worldly doors for her that way...Let those motivated by the love of Christ rather than the love of self choose wiser." (Peter Heck, Peterheck.com, September 1, 2017)

"No Christian truly committed to the faith could object to the wording of the Nashville Statement." (Erick Erickson,

Twitter.com, August 29, 2017)

I've a concern about the responses of my Christian brothers and sisters, many of whom have encouraged my own faith in their writings and who love God more than I do, I'm sure. So, what's my concern? The responses of these good-hearted people seem to shut off any opportunity for partly wrong people to work together to figure out where each may be wrong. One factor that always works against transformative dialogue is judging the motives of others.

Judging motives. We all do it, but is that wrong? Is that bad? The word "judge" has a range of meaning, one of which is "to assess." Assessing motives is natural and unavoidable. We are—all of us—detectives at heart, or motive police. This isn't a bad thing. When we see a person's action, we invariably consider why, often unconsciously. We're wired to ask why.

In our home, my wife usually gives me a "good night" and "I love you" before she goes to bed, but one night she doesn't. Without any conscious decision, an internal computer works to figure out why. There are a range of options: She's terribly tired and sleepy. She's feeling really sad and depressed. She's pissed off at me. She's feeling a bit ill. She's forgetful (we are, after all, well into our 50's now). Take a moment to think of other possibilities.

A crack member of the motive police, I choose one of the possibilities. I then draw a conclusion, and here's where it often gets criminal. For me, there's this disturbing magnetic pull to the darkest option. So my conclusion is likely to be: She's angry, and she's sending me that "silent treatment" message. Having determined her motive, I'll find myself mentally responding to it. "Oh, so *that's* how it is." Or "That's *so* immature" or "Well, I don't have to say anything to you when I go to bed either" or (fill in your own suggestion). My response will usually impact on our next morning specifically and our marriage generally. Not in a good way.

Assessing motive is a normal, helpful part of being human. But notice that I've done far more than simply assess. I've concluded what her motive was, I've assumed I was right, and I've treated her accordingly—some combination of anger, isolation, and pride. Not good. This judgment of motive divides, wounds, and stunts growth. It discourages dialogue and undermines relationship. It hurts both me and the other. And it keeps partly wrong people firmly entrenched in where they're wrong.

I go back to the Nashville statement. Both the critics of the statement and the critics of the critics are motivated by something. There are an array of options for us to choose. I immediately feel the negative ones rise to the top: That person is grasping at control. That person loves the praise of people more than the praise of God. That person hates gays. That person's insecure. That person's prejudiced.

But there's another possibility, isn't there? Like this one: That's a person like me who deeply loves God and is trying to figure out what God's heart for human flourishing is, but like me, they sometimes get things wrong. Why don't I assume and embrace that beautiful motive first? (Don't answer that! It's a trick question.)

Assuming the best is exactly where God wants us partly wrong people to start. I Corinthians 13:7 reminds us that love "believeth all things" (KJV) or "love trusts." (NIV) Love believes the best motive, which is closely tied to the chapter's uncomfortable reminders that love "keeps no record of wrongs and is not easily angered" (NIV). This love that believes the best motive opens the door for so much good.

But Roger, sometimes people's motives *are* broken and unhealthy. Of course they are, as I know well from observing my own heart. Neither you nor I, however, is in the position to know anyone's motives as God does. Remember, we're partly wrong. More than that, negative motive assessments are typically destructive. There's a reason why God calls us to believe the best motive. It's better to believe the best about someone and be wrong than to believe the worst and be right. When people's ideas or motives are flawed, they're most likely to change in the context of a community where the best is believed about them.

Isn't that true about you? How open to conversation and change are you when people say things like:

I knew you'd get it wrong.
You always just look out for yourself.
You only do things to impress people.
You'll never change.
I told her you'd forget, and I was right.
You're just a bigot.

Those kinds of words shut me down. Beat me down. End any conversation. Any civil conversation. And my partly wrong isn't likely to change. When we assume the worst about people, we make it less likely for their partly wrong to be changed.

I come back one final time to the Nashville Statement. The statement broaches some subjects that Christians desperately need to discuss together to better understand the heart of God and where each of us is wrong. That'll begin with believing the very best motives about people who hold a different position than our own.

When we embrace a negative motive narrative, these vital conversations just won't happen. Others won't want to learn anything from us, and we'll conclude we've nothing to learn from them. We'll stay more ignorant, missing the opportunity to learn where we may be wrong. We'll stay more arrogant—certain that we know people's motives and can't possibly be wrong.

Signers of the Nashville Statement like John Piper and Francis Chan and Jackie Hill-Perry have influenced me for good. Critics of the statement like Brian McLaren and Jen Hatmaker and Shaine Claiborne are writers whose words have influenced me for good. I need them all. We all need what they have to say. We all need to be in dialogue together, seeking to hear God in community rather than retreating to increasingly smaller circles where people believe mostly like I do. I'm not saying that we'll end up agreeing on everything, but we'll grow wiser in the dialogue, and we'll reflect a grace and unity our world desperately needs to see and know.

It's better to believe the best about someone and be wrong than to believe the worst and be right. And when we believe the best, we open the door to vital conversations that can help us all get a bit more right.

***

I hate for people to assume I have an ugly motive, which they can't see, but sometimes I make ugly choices, which they can clearly see. And sometimes, it's all they choose to see.

Chapter Twenty-One

***

WHEN YOUR FAILURE IS ALL PEOPLE SEE

Thomas Jefferson. Robert E. Lee. Thomas Yawkey.

What do those three men have in common? Besides being dead? Well, in 2017, they spent some time in the news. Jefferson, the slave owner. Yawkey, the Red Sox baseball owner who adamantly resisted integration. Lee, a general in the Confederate army. Deceased, their names were resurrected in op-ed pieces, news stories, television commentary and blogs. A verdict was rendered. They're wrong. They're racists. They're bad guys.

The proposed removal of a statue of Robert E. Lee was at the center of the fatal clash of white supremacist demonstrators, counter-demonstrators and Antifa in Charlottesville, VA in August of that year. New voices began calling for statues of Thomas Jefferson to be removed. John Henry, the current owner of the Red Sox baseball team, shortly thereafter called for the renaming of Yawkey Way, a street I have walked on my way to Boston's Fenway Park. So, why the call to remove their statues and pull their names from street signs? Because they were racists.

I'm glad we are talking about racism. Very glad. The Bible condemns it. Racism is an evil, and it should be named and condemned. We don't want to celebrate it. We don't want to encourage it. Symbols like monuments and street names and statues have a weight and influence to them, and it's legitimate to question if certain ones should remain.

In the noble fight against racism and other evils, however, we risk making a dangerous—perhaps fatal—judgment, namely this: A person's entire identity is defined solely by her worst behavior. We can reduce a partly wrong person to nothing but his wrong.

I've seen this when it comes to felons. That's the label we give them. Felons. I dislike the term because of what we do with it. "Felon" could simply mean "one who's committed a felony" but we struggle to leave it there. The label subtly becomes a slur that sums up the person's life and identity. Felon. The worst thing the person has done becomes their core identity. "You know she's a felon, don't you?" "We can't risk hiring him because he's a felon." Any other good the person is or does is buried under the label "felon." All we want to see—or choose to see—is felon. It's all or nothing.

Labels have that "all or nothing" gravitational pull. The pull invariably creates a kind of separation. There are bad people like felons, and there are good people, like me, who haven't done the felony thing. Good guys and bad guys. You're one or the other. No middle ground. This happens all the time with those who have, in a misguided moment, committed a felony. This all-or-nothing labeling breaks God's heart. In good moments, it breaks mine.

Some of you share my concern about how we characterize "felons." But are we doing the same thing with racists? Jefferson and Yawkey and Lee had racist attitudes and behaviors. Jefferson owned slaves and likely fathered children by one of them. Lee, too, was a slaveowner and defender of the Confederacy. Yawkey's team, the Boston Red Sox, was the last MLB team to integrate, reluctantly so. We need to call their behavior out. We need to name the evil. It's fair to use the term racist, but is it fair to summarize their entire identity by that? Is it fair to bury any good they did under the singular label "racist?"

Is that their only identity? Jefferson was a brilliant statesman who helped to craft our American democracy. Do we bury that entirely under his sins of slavery? Yawkey was a philanthropist whose foundation today helps families across all racial lines. Do we simply bury that under his racism as if it doesn't exist? That's easy and tempting, but is it fair? Is it how we wish to be treated...to have our lives singularly defined by our worst behaviors?

And doesn't racism develop in good people? Like you or me? In the aftermath of Charlottesville, President Obama tweeted: "No one is born hating another person because of the color of his skin or his background or his religion," (Twitter.com, August 12, 2017) a loose quote of Nelson Mandela. It garnered the single most likes of any tweet in Twitter history, 3.8 million likes. But if his statement is true, doesn't it beg a certain grace for the Jeffersons and

Yawkey's, who were influenced by their own parents and culture? Were they not also good kids who were influenced by the significant people in their lives? Again, is it fair to ignore our own mantras and make their racism the sum of their lives?

I have asked if it's fair. I will also ask if it's healthy. Is it good for the world? Is it good for Charlottesville? Is it good for us? Is it good to label the bad people, like felons and racists and white supremacists and Antifa and to then distinguish them from the "good people" like us? Does this "all or nothing" labeling and separating help us actually fight racism or does it end up dividing us, corrupting us and ultimately condemning us all?

The Bible soberly reminds us that *"all have sinned and fall short of the glory of God..." (Romans 3:23)* The reality is that all of us are a mix of good and evil, and all of us need the forgiveness of God and the righteousness of Jesus. This singular labeling of the "good" and the "bad" blinds us to the evil in us, inflates arrogance, and builds walls between us. This quest to identify those bad guys, to label them, to shame them and eliminate them is its own kind of evil. It's also self-defeating. After all, once we get rid of all the bad guys, who's left?

I think some statues need to be toppled, but if in the tearing down, I'm erecting the idea that people should be defined solely by their worst behavior, eventually the demolition crews will be coming for me. Nobody escapes that wrecking ball. As Jesus soberly warned: *"For in the same way you judge others, you will be judged, and with the measure you use, it will be measured to you."* *(Matthew 7:2)*

It's another way of saying, "what goes around, comes around." And once we've justified defining partly wrong people solely by their wrongs, the day will come when we'ill find that our wrongs are all that people choose to see in us. We, who today ostracize, will one day be the ostracized, identified solely by our sin. In her song, *Fallen,* Sarah McLachlan laments the "missed step" that has left her unredeemable, rejected even by former friends, who turn their heads away. Alas, what goes around, comes around.

No one escapes. But God offers a wonderful promise to the fallen and labeled and ostracized:

Do not be deceived: Neither the sexually immoral nor idolaters nor adulterers nor men who have sex with men nor thieves nor the greedy nor drunkards nor slanderers nor swindlers will inherit the kingdom of God. And that is what some of you were. But you were washed, you were sanctified, you were justified in the name of the Lord Jesus Christ and by the Spirit of our God. (1 Corinthians 6:9-11)

"And that is what some of you were." That's all people could see in you. That missed step. That sin. That failure. You were buried under a label, but God gifts you a new identity.

Fallen, but forgiven.
Racist, but redeemed.
Swindler, but saved.
Cheater, but cleansed.
Liar, but loved.
Addict, but accepted.

Yes, Sarah, there's a way to be redeemed. Jesus has made it possible. God sees the beauty beyond our failures. Shouldn't we do the same for others? Indeed, we must. Because God sees in us the beauty behind the beast. Because we don't want to be identified solely by our worst behavior. Because God will judge us as we have judged others. Because Jesus said to *"love each other as I have loved you." (John 15:12)*

***

I love a good game night. Except when I'm losing. Or when the night gets awkward and God insists on teaching me some life lesson out of it.

Chapter Twenty-Two

***

THAT WRONG BIBLE IDEA YOUR FRIEND BELIEVES

We were looking forward to a fun night together with our new friends, a pastor and his wife who lived in the town where we'd moved to start a church. We'd visited their church to learn more about the area, I'd chatted with him a bit, and my wife had connected with his wife. They invited us to their home to enjoy a meal, followed by a game.

What game to play? How about a fun little game of *Scruples*, harmlessly subtitled "The Game of Moral

Dilemmas"? Players are confronted with a hypothetical situation that forces a moral decision: "You accidentally damage a car in a parking lot. Do you leave a note with your name and phone number?" You then guess whether another player would answer *yes, no,* or *depends.* The best guesser wins. We'd enjoy a delightful evening.

I wish I could remember what the first question was, but it was obvious that the only possible answer for a God-loving pastor would be "no," so I guessed that as my friend's answer. This game would be easy. But he answered "yes." I was stunned. A few more shocking yeses and depends, and it was all too clear. My pastor friend was a moral infant. On those carded questions, there was a clearcut right answer, and he kept missing them. I'm guessing he was equally disturbed about my erratic moral compass.

Scruples is a clever game that flows out of real-life dilemmas in life. It also mirrors a dilemma that faces every person who believes that the Bible provides God's moral map for life. When faced with a moral question, the believer will go to the Bible to see God's heart in the matter and whether His answer is yes, no, or depends.

Some of you may be wondering whether the Bible actually has an "it depends" option. One Bible passage suggests it does:

"Accept the one whose faith is weak, without quarreling over disputable matters. One person's faith allows them to eat anything, but another, whose faith is weak, eats only vegetables. The one who eats everything must not treat with contempt the one who does not, and the one who does not eat everything must not judge the one who does, for God has accepted them. Who are you to judge someone else's servant? To their own master, servants stand or fall. And they will stand, for the Lord is able to make them stand.One person considers one day more sacred than another; another considers every day alike. Each of them should be fully convinced in their own mind." (Romans 14:1-4)

There are "disputable matters." Sometimes one person's faith allows them to do something that another person's faith doesn't. It depends on what they believe. It depends. Naturally, this complicates everything. A cynic might ask if this passage itself is disputable! But for those who acknowledge that some Bible teachings are disputable— what some would call gray areas—you have the challenging task of discerning what teachings are black and white and what teachings are gray. Good luck with that.

So, we encounter real-life dilemmas, like: should I drink alcoholic beverages? Searching the pages of the Bible, some will say "absolutely not," while others will answer "it's fine" or "it depends." Should I enlist in the military where I may have to kill another person? Again, the answers come. Of course. Definitely not. It depends. Can the gift of forgiveness and a home in heaven, the Father's house, be forfeited or lost? I've heard all three Scruples answers to that question as well. Partly wrong followers of Jesus all check off different boxes.

And surely you've thought something like I did playing that game. I can't believe that anyone who loves God and His Word could draw any other conclusion than the one I've reached. It's so obvious. Playing the game, I was reminded of the real-life reality: Partly wrong people interpret the teachings of the Bible differently. We're right on some things and wrong on other things. Again, we just don't know which are which. I don't know where my pastor friend was right and where I was right.

I'd love to give you a three-point formula for determining the right interpretation of every single Bible teaching. Unfortunately, the Bible offers no such formula. But it does provide clear instruction for how partly wrong God-followers should live with their different understandings of

God's Word. I invite you first to go back to the Bible passage in Romans 14 above and to re-read that section. It contains three valuable guidelines for how partly wrong people should handle their conflicting understandings of the Bible, starting with this:

"Each of them should be fully convinced in their own mind." (Romans 14:5)

Each of us is called to go to God's Word, to reflect, to pray and to then make a decision as to what we believe God is saying. We need to arrive at a conclusion. Since God-loving people disagree, we may be tempted to think that no conclusions are wrong or that conclusions don't matter. Don't believe it. Some conclusions are right and some are wrong. God calls us to study His Word, discern its meaning and draw conclusions. We should seek out what is right even though we may be wrong.

In reflecting on what God is saying—in considering whether His word gives a yes, no, or depends—we should ask ourselves questions. Am I simply concluding what I've always been taught? Is my conclusion based on what I *want* to be true? How's my cultural setting influencing me? We should get counsel from others. Read. Have coffee with a friend. In all of it, we should be praying, asking God to give us direction. Then we need to draw a conclusion and begin living what we believe. We'll find that others disagree. So, how should we respond to them?

"The one who eats everything must not treat with contempt the one who does not..." (Romans 14:3)

Don't treat those who disagree with contempt. That word "contempt" sounds really strong, and it is. The online Oxford Dictionary defines: "Contempt: the feeling that a person or a thing is beneath consideration, worthless, or deserving scorn." (https://en.oxforddictionaries.com/definition/contempt) Those are strong words, but don't let them fool you into thinking you never go there. God's on to something. Contempt, however strong, is very subtle and easily undetected.

I've come to see how it bubbles up in me. When I'm having a conversation that surfaces a difference of opinion, I'll find it easy to "explain" their conclusion with a label. She disagrees with me on the race problem in America, and I'll find the word "racist" coming to mind. He disagrees with me on the role of women in ministry, and I'll find the word "misogynist" surfacing. The label may be bigot, intolerant, homophobe, liberal, conservative, elitist, socialist, fundamentalist, dogmatist, passivist.

Watch what happens when I assign the label. I dismiss the idea out of hand. Why? Because their interpretation is simply flowing out of their narrowness, evil, or blindness. It can't be a sincerely-weighed conclusion that may be right. It's a fundamentally flawed conclusion that can't possibly be right. Contempt: "beneath consideration." Their idea isn't even worth my thought. It's no longer simply a difference of opinion. It's a reflection of their brokenness. Therefore, I won't give their idea the time of day. Their conclusion isn't worth my time.

It's hard not to go a step further. THEY aren't worth my time. Contempt: Worthless. The racist or homophobe or fundamentalist that she is, I don't even want to be around her or her kind. In my anger and/or self-righteousness, I don't want to have discussions with them. Their ideas have no value. They're not worth my time. I'll move toward avoidance.

Contempt creates terrible losses: lost love, lost community, lost opportunity to learn. God, in His great love for us, warns that we not let contempt take root in our hearts. He warns of another evil root.

"...the one who does not eat everything must not judge the one who does, for God has accepted them." (Romans 14:3)

Don't judge those who disagree with you. Judgmentalism is a first cousin to contempt, but looks different enough to get its own warning label. When I encounter someone with a different opinion, I may find myself looking down at them. The person with a different view of spiritual gifts than mine just isn't as mature as I am. Their faith is weak. They're ignorant or simple or gullible or overly-sensitive or insecure.

In judging, I see their difference in opinion as a product, not of evil, but of weakness. I don't feel contempt for them. I feel pity for them. Bless their hearts. They're just simple. If contempt is assuming my character is superior, then judging is assuming my wisdom or insight is superior.

Judgment was what I initially felt rising up during our game of *Scruples*. The temptation isn't avoidance; it's arrogance. The temptation isn't despising them. It's patronizing them. It's not that you don't want to be around them (as with contempt), but you've no real sense you've anything to learn from them.

Judgment may not create physical distance, but it creates

spiritual distance. Though I may talk with you, I don't give your ideas any real credibility because you just don't have the wisdom or maturity that I have. We're not really on the same level. Cousin to contempt that it is, judgment creates similar losses: lost humility, lost community, and the lost opportunity to learn from another partly wrong friend. As such, it breaks God's heart.

God graciously allowed me to see, during a party game, my easy drift to judgment for people who see His Word differently than I. The pastor and his wife continued for years to be grace-giving friends. I'm pretty certain, however, that we never played *Scruples* again.

***

I'm honored—and still somewhat surprised—that you'd take the time to read my words, twenty-two chapters of them. But I've one final word for you, my fellow partly-wrong friend. Hint: You have something vital to say.

Chapter Twenty-Three

***

YOU CAN'T KEEP SILENT

In the summer of 1979, I enrolled in my very first college class: Speech 101. Many people dread speaking in public, but I liked it, and I was looking forward to this class. One of our first speech assignments was an informative speech, and I chose "How to bag groceries properly." (Cute, huh? It was my first job.) I gave my speech, sprinkled with humor, insight and clever illustrations.

I couldn't wait to see my grade sheet, that is, until I saw it.

I don't remember the actual grade, only that the teacher had written, in large letters at the bottom of the page, "You come across smug and cocky." I wasn't sure what those words meant, but they didn't sound bright and cheery. I looked them up. The dictionary wasn't flattering. Sigh.

How do you screw up a speech on bagging groceries?

This was one of my first reminders that speaking and writing is risky business. I've written and spoken many many times since then. I've offended people. I've made inaccurate statements. I've taught wrong ideas. I've been smug and cocky and judgmental. I've neglected key ideas. I've encouraged error. And I've felt many times what I felt after getting that grade sheet.

Why bother? Why take the risk of writing or saying anything? Maybe you've had some form of this question shut you down. Why blog? Why give advice? Why warn? Why teach? Why write a song? Why persuade? Why encourage? Why write a book? It's only an opportunity to screw things up.

In the moment, the logic makes sense. Because I might be wrong, I should never proclaim an idea. I should never make a claim. I should never teach. I should never promote or persuade. I should never coach or counsel or correct. I should just keep to myself.

Peter, our good friend in the pages of the Bible—our partly wrong poster child—was feeling this very thing. We read in John, Chapter 21 that Peter had gone back to his old job of fishing, to the quiet lake where he'd made an income for years. It was days after Jesus had died. Yes, Jesus had come back to life after three days dead, but Peter can't forget his own fatal words, thrice spoken: "I don't know the man."

Those unexpected, once thrilling, words of Jesus, "you are Peter and upon this rock I will build my church," are so faint that Peter now doubts Jesus actually said them. The only words Peter remembers are the ones he wishes he could take back:

Let's build three tabernacles.
You will never die, Lord.
You'll never wash my feet.
No, I am the greatest.
I will never deny you.
I don't know the man.

Honestly, it feels like every time he speaks, he just screws something up. Well, Peter can fix that problem. Just shut up and fish. Go back to something where you can't say the wrong thing, disappoint someone, harm people. If you don't say anything, you can't say the wrong thing. I've felt that. I've made so many bad choices. I've verbalized so many wrong ideas. Sometimes, I just want to move to a lakeside cabin deep in a New Hampshire forest. I've keenly felt Peter's pull to retreat.

So Peter is on the lake with his buddies, but the early results aren't encouraging. Fishing into the early morning hours, they catch nothing. Then a voice calls out from the shore, "Throw your net on the right side of the boat and you will find some." (John 21:6) However annoying the stranger's advice may have been for the seasoned fishermen, they take his advice and end up with a boatload of fish. Uh oh. They've seen this story before. The stranger on the shore is Jesus, and he's got bread and a breakfast fire kindled for their fish.

As they're finishing the meal, Jesus asks Peter if he loves him. Peter quietly affirms his love for Jesus, who then utters three beautiful, unexpected words that still bring tears to my eyes.

Feed my lambs.

Jesus asks him two more times, graciously providing Peter a moment to counter his three denials around another campfire. But each time Peter affirms his love, Jesus offers a final word to Peter that is perhaps more precious than "I love you, too."

Feed my lambs.
Take care of my sheep.
Feed my sheep. (21:15-17)

I hear in these words an invitation—no, a command—not to give up. Not to quit, not to hide behind fishing nets, not to stop speaking, not to retreat to a New Hampshire cabin. Peter, I want you, my dear partly wrong friend, to keep giving my words to others. Don't bail on me because I have not bailed on you. I trust you. Feed my sheep.

And I believe that Jesus is speaking those very same words to you and me. Feed my lambs. Take care of my sheep. Feed my sheep. Keep speaking words of grace to others. Keep encouraging. Keep teaching. Keep challenging. Keep warning. Keep sharing. Keep writing music. Keep thanking. Keep correcting. Even though your words will sometimes be wrong. Even though your attitudes will sometimes be wrong. Even though your choices will sometimes be wrong.

Outside of Jesus, God has only ever used partly wrong people to feed his sheep, to speak his words, to share his love. He wants you and me to feed his sheep.

That's the only reason why I stepped out to write a book. God uses partly wrong people to speak his words to others. I know that some parts of this book are wrong; I just don't know which parts they are, though you probably have an idea or two. I know I've made statements that I'll discover later to be mistaken. I know I'm a screw-up, but Jesus hasn't given me the option to retreat to a lonely cabin and to age in silence.

This is the only reason why I've ever stood up in front of people to teach something from the Bible. God loves to speak through partly wrong people. It's why I blog, why I write notes, why I tell people about Jesus, why I write poetry.

Because God says to partly wrong people like me: Feed my sheep. Encourage one another daily. Teach. Reprove. Exhort. Warn. Lead. Restore one another gently. Prophesy. Bless. Challenge.

God spoke through the prophet, Jonah, who hated his
audience and wanted them to die.

God spoke through Peter, who both rebuked and denied
Jesus.

God spoke through Roger, who cared little about the poor
for most of his life.

It's the plan of God to speak and work through partly
wrong people.

Of course you'll be wrong sometimes. Keep writing.

Of course you'll make mistakes. Keep speaking.

Of course you'll have wrong ideas. Keep teaching.

Of course you'll have mixed motives. Keep writing songs
and verse.

Of course you'll err. Keep blogging and posting.

God can fix and redeem and correct your flawed, mistaken
words. He's been in the business of doing that for a very
long time. There's no mess you make that He can't clean
up. Entrust your fallibility to his good hands. Oddly
enough, your fallibility makes you a better speaker and
writer. When recognized, it keeps you humble and
gracious. Owning your errors and talking about them, as
threatening as it feels, enhances your credibility. It models
healthy confession and trust in God, which people

desperately need to see in action.

Make no mistake. Your words matter. You should pray and ask God for help. You should listen to others and get counsel. You should choose your words carefully. Be "slow to speak," the Bible says (James 1:19). Be slow...but speak. We're all partly wrong, and we need to hear from other partly wrong people so that we can all get a little more right. God wants your voice to be heard. Peter began speaking once again. I've added my voice to the conversation. Now, it's your turn.

ACKNOWLEDGMENTS

I'm still shocked that this book was written. I had no lifetime dream of writing a book. I have never longed to hold a book with my name beneath the title. On a spring Sunday in 2015, I taught a message to a handful of people and had an unexpected nudge that it may be the seed for a book, which I really didn't want to write. But here it is today. So the obvious credit goes to God, Who asked me to trust His odd idea that I had something to say. God has poured untold (and often unrecognized) grace into my life, and I hope that this book points to His brilliance and compassion.

I wish I knew what parts of this book I got wrong, but I am trusting God to help you sort out the wheat from the weeds.

This book would never have come together without God, Who loved engaging a host of people to help make this book possible and better. My brother, Bruce Martin, was the incessant voice that I needed to be writing. He has invested countless hours helping me hone my ideas and understand the writing process. (And your life will be changed by reading his book, <u>Desperate for Hope</u>.) No one wanted to see this book written more than my wife, Joy, who believes in me and loves me irrationally. My son, Ben, periodically gave me the "stop talking about it and start writing" kick-in-the-butt, which got the train back on the rails more than once. Through regular phone conversations, Carrye Burr, my daughter, provided keen insight, timely encouragement, and tips she learned from writing her own amazing book, <u>How to Be a Moon</u>.

Carrye saved me from an enormous oversight. She advised that I needed people to help review the book. I was writing a book about partly wrong people desperately needing to learn from others, and I had no plan to enlist reviewers. Uh oh. Talk about partly wrong! Several people stepped up to review chapters for me, and the book is profoundly better and less wrong for their investment and insights: Brenda Thompson, Iris Reed, James Robinson, Jon Raddatz, Carlee MacDonald, Carrye Burr, Joy Martin, Bruce Martin, David Blackwell, Kathy Sanderson, Marie Griffin, and Alicia Yost.

Rob Abercrombie, part of a writing group which spurred me on, offered the creative idea for the cover photo, which was taken by my daughter, Rachel Martin-Raddatz. For those I have failed to acknowledge, forgive me. I am, after all, partly wrong.

PARTLY WRONG

Chapter Discussion Questions

Below are questions that may be used for personal reflection or group discussion of the book's 23 chapters. The questions are designed to help you wrestle with the book's ideas and to better understand yourself. For a group setting, their purpose is to help you get to know each other better and to create opportunities to learn from each other. You'll connect with some questions more than others, based on your personality or group dynamics. Use the questions that are most helpful; skip the others. The one question you can always ask is: "What idea in this chapter is partly wrong?"

Chapter One: It Sucks to Be Wrong

Fun Opener: Why did you buy or begin reading this book?

Word association game: What is the first word that comes to mind when you hear the word "failure"?

Some of our mistakes and failures are more memorable than others. What personal story (or two) comes immediately come to mind?

What do you dislike most about being wrong?

We all respond to our failures and wrongs in different ways: hiding them, ignoring them, dismissing them, laughing them off, denying them, fixing them, withdrawing, blaming and more. What response do you move toward more readily, or does it vary from situation to situation?

What emotional responses do you typically have to failure or mistakes? Anger, sadness, discouragement, guilt, shame, despair, embarrassment, joy, other: _____?

Brainstorm the names of people in the Bible who made mistakes or had wrong ideas.

Chapter Two: It Rocks to be Right

Fun Opener: What class or topic did you enjoy most in school? Enjoy the least?

In class settings, are you eager to give answers, hesitant to give answers or something in between? Why?

If you were Peter when he gave the right answer and got the affirmation of Jesus, what would you have enjoyed most about that moment? (Good, bad or ugly!)

Can you remember a particular classroom setting where you said or did the wrong thing?

(Read Matthew 16:13-23)
A key point Roger makes is that everyone is partly wrong all the time. Do you agree or disagree?

Do you find Peter's story to be encouraging or discouraging?

Does anything stand out to you about how Jesus interacts with Peter and the other disciples in this story?

Why do you think Jesus calls Peter "Satan?"

Why do you think God included this story in the Bible?

Chapter Three: I Did Not See That Coming

Fun Opener: How many different houses or apartments have you lived in? How many countries and/or states?

Do you have a story like Roger's of a mistaken idea that did or could have had serious consequences?

Is having incomplete knowledge the same as being wrong?

(Read 2 Peter 3:18 and Colossians 1:9-10)
We all need to grow, and Roger says this is simply another way of saying that we're all wrong. Do you agree or disagree?

What are some of the ways in which God helps us to grow? What are some "tools" He uses?

Why is our growth so important to God?

Chapter Four: Ignorance Is Bless

Fun Opener: What is a water sport or activity you really enjoy?

Word Association: What word first comes to mind when you hear the word "ignorant"?

How is ignorance different than stupidity? Or is it different?

What is an activity or skill or event that you may know more about than the average person? Now, name one you know less about.

Why is it so hard to reveal or admit that we don't know something?

Why is it hard to ask someone else for help? (Ignore this question if you *love* asking for help.)

(Read Psalm 19:7-14)
What are some of the benefits of reading and reflecting on

God's words in the Bible?

What are some ways in which God teaches us things or speaks to us through other people?

Chapter Five: The Broken People God Uses

Fun Opener: What is the first paying job you had? What are some of the jobs you have worked since then?

In the pages of the Bible, God uses some pretty messed up people for good. Which person's story is very troubling or perplexing to you?   Which person's story is very encouraging?

(Read 2 Corinthians 4:5-18)
Why does God work through flawed people?

What benefits or advantages might there be for God to do His good work through broken people?

Some suggest that a leader or teacher should not expose their own struggles, doubts or weaknesses. Do you agree? What are the benefits of sharing struggles? What are the risks?

Chapter Six: What's Wrong with the World?

Fun Opener: Name a place in the world that you'd really like to visit. Name a place in the world you definitely don't wish to visit. Why?

There are many tragic evils, abuses and injustices in our world. What are some that particularly burden your heart?

What are some ways in which Christians are working against the darkness, evil and suffering in our world?

What are some ways in which Christians are part of, or are

contributing to, the darkness of our world?

(Read Matthew 5:13-16)
What, if any, are the similarities between salt and light?

What does it mean to for Christians to "let your light shine before others"? What does that look like?

What does "covering" or "hiding" the light look like? Give possible examples.

Chapter Seven: Facebook Wars and the Death of Dialogue

Fun Opener: What social networking sites do you visit or have an account for? Which one(s) do you access most often and why?

Agree or disagree with this statement: It is extremely difficult to have any kind of civil dialogue on most social media outlets. Or replace the words "extremely difficult" with ones of your own choosing.

Do you think that Roger came down a bit too hard on debate?

In what ways does win/lose thinking work against dialogue, learning and relationships?

(Read James 1:19-20)
What does it mean to be "swift to hear"? Why is that so difficult? What might "swift to hear" look like in practice?

What action steps can we take to be "slow to speak"?

Is anger a bad thing? When does anger work against the righteousness God desires? What can we do to slow down or appropriately direct our anger?

Chapter Eight: I've Nothing to Learn from You

Fun Opener: Rank the following five activities in order of what you enjoy most: Read a book, play a game, listen to music/go to a concert, take in a movie, watch T.V. (For fun, the five are listed in Roger's order of enjoyment.)

Can you recall books, music, activities, or entertainment that were either discouraged or banned for you in your family, school, church or country?

When might it be healthy or advisable to discourage someone from reading some material or author? When is it unhealthy?

(Read Acts 17:1-12)
What are some elements of Paul's message that would be uncomfortable or offensive for his listeners both in Thessalonica and Berea?

Which is more surprising to you—the violent antagonism of some in Thessalonica or the willingness of so many in Berea to consider radical new ideas?

Are there times when you've avoided listening to certain ideas or speakers because you didn't want them to be right? Examples: political ideas, spiritual/religious ideas, relationship ideas, or financial ideas. What are (or were) the consequences of such avoidance?

Chapter Nine: What Sodom Got Wrong

Fun Opener: What are some things people rank? Can you think of an award (certificate, trophy, ribbon, commendation, prize, medal) you've gotten?

How would you define sin? What makes an attitude, thought, word or action "wrong"?

What are some reasons why we rank sins as to their seriousness?

Is there any good reason to rank sins?

What are the dangers of ranking sins?

(Read Proverbs 6:16-19 and Ezekiel 16:49-51)
What do these Bible passages reveal about the heart of God?

What are some wrong behaviors and attitudes that people tend to minimize or dismiss entirely?

Chapter Ten: The Perfect Church

Fun Opener: How many different church denominations can you name? What kind of churches have you been part of?

What were some of the weaknesses and struggles of the churches described in the New Testament?

What are some of the weaknesses and struggles of churches in America today?

(Read Romans 12:3-13)
What are some things that members of a church community ought to be doing for each other?

The Bible describes a church community as a body or a family which needs the care and gifts of each member. Should this reality cause Christians to pause longer over, and take more seriously, the decision to leave one church for another? What are some healthy reasons for leaving a church? What are some unhealthy reasons?

What steps could churches take to engage with and learn from other churches?

Chapter Eleven: America's Most Dangerous Person

Fun Opener: Share something you've done or been part of that may be considered dangerous?

In what occupations might someone need to point out dangerous ideas?

Is there ever a place for identifying a dangerous person? If so, why? And how could that be done in a healthy way?

(Read Matthew 7:1-5)
What is the main point Jesus is making with His word about planks and sawdust?

What might Jesus' instruction look like in action? How does one actually "take the plank out of your own eye"?

What kind(s) of judging is healthy and what kind(s) isn't?

Chapter Twelve: Monsters Like Me

Fun Opener: Name some famous movie villains and monsters.

What's one of the worst slurs you've received or names you've been called?

What emotions stirred in you when you first heard about the Brock Turner story or when you read it in this chapter?

Do you agree or disagree with this statement: Every adult who has ever lived has done something shameful.

(Read John 8:2-11)
What's wrong/evil about what the Pharisees and teachers of the

law are doing here?

Jesus said, "Let any one of you who is without sin be the first to throw a stone at her." Does this mean we shouldn't name or identify wrong behavior? Does it mean that wrong behavior should never be punished? What is the point of this word from Jesus?

Do you believe there are times when people out to be publicly shamed for their behavior? If so, why? When? And how?

How do we find the way to name evil and take it seriously without becoming self-righteous, hypocritical and hateful? What can we learn from how Jesus responded here?

Chapter Thirteen: Of Course Parents Are Screwy

Fun Opener: How many brothers and sisters do you have? What are their names, and what's the birth order?

What are some graces you received from your dad or mom? What's something you wished they had done differently?

Why are the failures and mistakes of parents so difficult for them to forget or forgive?

(Read Proverbs 22:6. If possible, read it in more than one Bible version.)
What's encouraging about this proverb? What's potentially troubling about this proverb?

How much responsibility do parents have for the struggles or failures of their children?

What are some ways in which the failures, mistakes and struggles of parents can create an opportunity for good or growth in their children?

Should parents share their past struggles (failures, addictions, bad decisions) with their children? What are the benefits? What are the risks?

Chapter Fourteen: When God Agrees with You on Everything

Fun Opener: Can you name a family rule or chore or practice that you didn't like as a child (age 3-17)? Perhaps you can think of more than one:)

Word association: What word first comes to mind when you hear the word "repent"?

In your own words, how would you define "repentance"?

Roger describes repentance as a regular choice Christians are called to make, while others would suggest it's a fundamental one-time decision. Which way would you lean and why?

Why is it so hard to repent?

(Read Exodus 20:1-17)
Which of the Ten Commandments is most surprising to you and why?

Which of the Ten Commandments do you find challenging to obey?

What are some of God's commands or teachings that you've struggled to understand or perhaps even accept as good?

Chapter Fifteen: The One Time You're Always Right

Fun Opener: Roughly how many loans have you gotten in your lifetime? What loan story is especially interesting or memorable? Has anyone ever forgiven a loan or helped you in making payments?

What are some of the thoughts you had or emotions you felt while reading the Rusty Woomer story in this chapter?

(Read Matthew 18:21-33)
Based on this passage and other Bible instructions, how would you define forgiveness?

What are some common misconceptions about forgiveness?

For some offenses, you may have to choose to forgive someone every day of your life. Do you agree or disagree with this statement, and why?

What about this story do you find hard to understand or follow?

Is there a specific forgiveness struggle you'd like others in your group to pray with you about?

Chapter Sixteen: I Humbly Admit that You're Wrong

Fun Opener: What are the names of some people you've worked for or under? Which one(s) did you like best, and why? Have you ever had an employer who admitted he/she was wrong?

Why is it so hard to admit that we're wrong?

Is it possible to apologize without ever actually taking responsibility for our wrong action?

(Read John 9:24-41)
What different kinds of blindness show up in this story?

In what way are the religious leaders blind? Why is their blindness so serious?

If we really believed that we might be wrong, how would it change how we act? Or how we talk to people who disagree with us? Or how we discuss controversial ideas?

Do we lose credibility with people when we acknowledge that we may be wrong? Who or why not?

Chapter Seventeen: Stupid Makes You Humble

Fun Opener: Can you think of predictions you made (sports score, TV show, political winner, investment, movie awards, etc) that turned out to be wrong?

What do you particularly dislike about making a claim or prediction that's wrong? Or do you love being wrong, announcing it often to others?

How would you define humility?

(Read 1 Corinthians 1:26-31)
God chooses the weak and foolish and lowly and despised. Can you think of people God used in the Bible who fit one of these descriptors?

Why do you think God uses such people?

What kind of good things might God do through our ignorance or us looking foolish? For others? For us?

Do you think God allows our ignorance to be exposed in a gracious attempt to save us?

Chapter Eighteen: Let's Talk About Jesus

Fun Opener: What are some fears or phobias you have? Based on such concerns, what kinds of jobs would you avoid at all costs?

Do you believe that all Christians are called by God to share the good news of Jesus and invite others to trust Him? Why or why not? What Bible instructions support your conclusion?

What are some reasons why Christians struggle or fail to share the good news of Jesus with others?

What are some reasons why people are uncomfortable with someone talking to them about Jesus?

(Read 1 Peter 3:15)
What stands out in this verse about how we are to share with others the reason for our hope?

What does it look like to share our hope with gentleness and respect? What kinds of actions or words or approaches might be ruled out by this call to share with gentleness and respect?

Roger has emphasized that we've something to learn from every person we encounter. Do you agree? How might such a belief change how we talk to people as we share our hope in Jesus?

Does a listening, learning posture enhance our ability to share hope, or does it dilute it?

Chapter Nineteen: How Right Must You Be?

Fun Opener: What are some jobs that require a high degree of precision and accuracy?

The chapter raises the question of what core things must be believed, embraced or done in order for someone to enter the kingdom of heaven. What are the possible advantages of asking such a question? What are the possible dangers?

Are we more likely to overestimate or underestimate what must happen for someone to enter the kingdom of heaven?

What reality of the "Good News" significantly influenced your decision to love and trust God? (If applicable)

What part(s) of this chapter is partly wrong?

What biblical truth should've been mentioned or more emphasized in this chapter?

(Read 1 Corinthians 15:1-11)
When Paul talks about key features of the gospel here, what are some things you're surprised he doesn't mention? Things you're surprised he does mention?

What's the relationship between facts and faith? Between believing facts and trusting a person?

Chapter Twenty: The Motive Police

Fun Opener: What detective books, shows, or detective games do you like and why? Describe any job you've had that involved diagnosing or trouble-shooting a problem.

All of us persistently try to figure out the "why" behind things that happen. Why do you think we're obsessed with why?

(Read 1 Corinthians 4:1-5)
Is it ever possible to determine the motive behind someone's choice?

God clarifies here that He will one day judge our motives. What do you think that means? How is the word "judge" being used?

Do you think there is any time when it's healthy or right for us to judge the motives of others?

Roger says that "it's better to believe the best about someone and be wrong than to believe the worst and be right." Do you agree or disagree? Why?

How can believing the best about people's motives nurture healthy relationships and growth?

Chapter Twenty-One: When Your Failure Is All People See

Fun Opener: What kinds of competitions, teams or groups (debate, sports, quiz, musical, choral, 4H, speaker, gaming, cheerleading, etc) have you been a part of? Can you think of a memorable loss you or your team experienced?

Across the country, there has been a move to remove Confederate monuments and symbols that are seen by some to represent hate, prejudice and racism. Do you think this is a good idea? Why or why not?

We use labels for people all the time, labels like conservative, liberal, racist, felon, liar, bigot, optimist, pessimist, fundamentalist, pacifist. What are some other labels that we give to people? How can such labels be used in a way that is helpful? In a way that is harmful?

(Read Luke 6:27-38)
From this passage, what are the dangers or problems with identifying other people solely by their worst behavior or decisions?

When we extend grace or mercy to people's failures and sins, does that dilute the seriousness of their choices?

How does our culture's growing tendency to shame and shun "sinners" create a fresh opportunity for us to share the hope of grace through Jesus? What's the message of hope that might especially resonate in a "graceless" culture?

Chapter Twenty-Two: That Wrong Bible Idea Your Friend Believes

Fun Opener: What are some issues people passionately disagree over? (If you dare, pick one issue and have each person briefly share his/her viewpoint.)

How is it that Christians can draw very different conclusions when reading the same Bible passages?

(Read Romans 14:1-12)
This passage addresses "disputable matters." How does one identify what matters are disputable? Do these verses provide any helpful clues in making that determination?

What are some issues that you believe are "disputable matters," and why?

Why do our disagreements with others stir strong emotions at times?

When someone disagrees with us about a Bible instruction or a cultural issue, what are some unhealthy attitudes and responses that can surface?

How do we live in the tension between making judgments about Bible teachings without judging people who arrive at different conclusions? What judging is healthy and what judging isn't?

Chapter Twenty-Three: You Can't Be Silent

Fun Opener: Rate the following communication mediums in the order of what you most like using? [Phone call, text, chat, messaging, video call(Skype, etc.), personal conversation, email, letter, telegram]

What are some of the things that can "go wrong" when we are

speaking to others? What kinds of damage can we do with our words? What kinds of unintentional harm can come from our words?

The Bible highlights multiple times in which Peter said something that he later regretted, and Roger lists several of those statements in this chapter. Is there an incident or two with which you can relate, and why?

(Read John 21:1-17)
It appears that Peter, haunted by his failures, had given up on being used by God any more. Have you had a similar experience that you feel comfortable sharing?

What do you learn about the heart and plan of Jesus from this story?

What part of this story is most meaningful to you, and why?

Jesus encourages the disheartened Peter to once again step up to serve and bless others with his words. Is there reason to believe that this instruction is for all followers of Jesus and not just Peter? Can you think of similar kinds of instructions or encouragement to other people in the Bible?

How do you believe God wants you to use your words to bless others?